REVIEW FOR THE
CLEP* GENERAL HUMANITIES
EXAMINATION

Complete review of skills

By
Brian Eckert

comex systems, inc.
5 Cold Hill Rd.
Suite 24
Mendham, NJ 07945

© Copyright 1978, 1980, 1981, 1982, 1987, 1989, 1990, 1991, 1993, 1994,1996, 1998, 1999, 2001, 2003, 2005, 2006

Published by

comex systems, inc.
5 Cold Hill Rd.
Suite 24
Mendham, NJ 07945

ISBN 1-56030-138-4

CLEP* (College Level Examination Program)

CLEP provides a way to determine the level of knowledge you now have in relation to college level material. CLEP does not determine your ability to learn a subject. People tend to have a low evaluation of their ability. There is no way you can determine your present level unless you take the examination. You can save time and money taking these examinations to earn credit.

WHY DID WE WRITE THIS BOOK?

Our firm has conducted many classroom reviews for CLEP General Examinations. Our instructors have assisted thousands of candidates. From this experience we have determined that:

1. In each area there is specific material beneficial for candidates to know.

2. There is a need for a simple-to-follow review book which helps students improve their ability to achieve.

3. It is important for students to become accustomed to the specific directions found on the examination before taking the examination.

4. It is beneficial to develop a systematic approach to taking an objective examination.

This book will help you perform at your highest potential so that you can receive your best score.

The flyers "CLEP COLLEGES" (Listing where you can take the CLEP tests and the colleges that accept credit) and "CLEP INFORMATION FOR CANDIDATES" are available free by calling (800) 257-9558, by writing to: CLEP, PO Box 6600, Princeton, NJ 08541-6600 or online at www.collegeboard.com.

CLEP INFORMATION

WHAT IS CLEP GENERAL?

CLEP is a nation-wide program of testing which began in 1965. Today thousands of colleges recognize CLEP as a way students can earn college credit. Each year hundreds of thousands of students take CLEP examinations. The testing program is based on the theory that "**what** a person knows is more important than **how** he has learned it." All examinations are designed and scored by the College Entrance Examination Board (CEEB). The purpose of each examination is to determine whether your current knowledge in a subject can qualify you for credit in that area at a particular college.

There are five general examinations. The subject areas are:

1.   English Composition
2.   Mathematics
3.   Social Science / History
4.   Natural Science
5.   Humanities

Credits earned through achieving on these examinations replace basic liberal arts credits which are required by many colleges. Each of these general examinations is very broad in coverage. Questions are from the wide range of subjects included in each of the major disciplines. The General CLEP Humanities Examination will include questions related to literature, music and art. Because of the broad coverage in each examination, you are not expected to be knowledgeable in all areas. There will be some questions on all the tests you will not be able to answer.

HOW LONG ARE THE EXAMINATIONS?

Each CLEP General Examination is 1½ hours in length. Each examination is divided into separate timed portions.

HOW MUCH DO THE EXAMINATIONS COST?

Currently, the fee to take each examination is $50.00. They may be taken one at a time or in any combination. (NOTE: Fees change periodically.)

WHERE CAN THE EXAMINATIONS BE TAKEN?

The CEEB (College Entrance Examination Board) has designated certain schools in each state to serve as test centers for CLEP examinations. The same examinations are given at all test centers. If you are a member of the armed forces, check with the Education Services Officer at your base. Special testings are set up for military personnel. A list of test centers may be found at www.collegeboard.com.

WHEN ARE THE TESTS GIVEN?

Most CLEP examinations are administered during the third week of every month except December and February. The test center chooses the day of the week. A few test centers administer the tests by appointment only. Check with the center where you will take the test for specific information. If you are serving with the United States Military, check with the Education Services Officer at your base to find out about the DANTES testing program. You will be given information about testing as applicable to military personnel.

HOW DO YOU REGISTER FOR AN EXAMINATION?

A standard registration form may be obtained from the test center where you plan to take the examination. Many centers require that you register (send registration form and fee for examinations to be taken) a month prior to your selected date.

WHEN WILL SCORES BE RECEIVED?

When you take most of the tests on the computer you will receive your score immediately (the English Composition with Essay must be graded first). If you are in the military and are taking the test on paper it will take up to 6 weeks to receive your scores. You can also request that a copy be sent to a college. The score you receive will be a scaled score. CEEB keeps a record of your scores on file for 20 years. You can obtain an additional copy or have a copy sent to a college if you contact:

College Board
PO BOX 6600
ATTN: Transcript Service
Princeton, NJ 08541
800-257-9558

IS IT NECESSARY TO BE ENROLLED IN A COLLEGE BEFORE YOU TAKE AN EXAMINATION?

Each college has established policies regarding CLEP. Check with the school you wish to attend. Many schools do not require enrollment before taking CLEP examinations.

HOW MANY CREDITS CAN BE EARNED?

Each college determines the number of credits that can be earned by CLEP examinations. Most colleges award six credits for achievement on a CLEP General Examination.

HOW ARE THE EXAMS SCORED?

See page VII for a detailed explanation of scoring.

HOW ARE THE SCORES EVALUATED?

The examinations are administered to college students who are taking a course the examination credits will replace. These students do not take the examination for credit. They take it to establish a standard by which your score can be evaluated. Percentile levels of achievement are determined. For example, if you score at the 25th percentile, this would indicate that you achieved as well as the **bottom** 25 percent of those students who took that examination to set a standard.

There is no correlation between the number of questions you answer correctly and the percentile level you achieve. The number would vary from test to test.

CAN THE SAME SCORES EARN A DIFFERENT NUMBER OF CREDITS AT DIFFERENT SCHOOLS?

Yes, different schools may require different levels of achievement. Your scores may earn more credits at one institution than at another. For example: if you achieve at the 25th percentile level, you could earn credit at a school which required the 25th percentile level; you could not earn credit at a school which required a higher level of achievement.

CAN CLEP CREDITS BE TRANSFERRED?

Yes, provided the school to which you transfer recognizes CLEP as a way to earn credit. Your scores will be evaluated according to the new school's policy.

CAN AN EXAMINATION BE RETAKEN?

Many schools allow you to retake an examination if you did not achieve the first time. Some do not. Check your particular school's policy before you retake an examination. Be realistic, if you almost achieved the level at which you could earn credit, do retake the examination. If your score was quite low, take the course it was designed to replace.

IF YOU DECIDE TO RETAKE AN EXAMINATION, six months must elapse before you do so. Scores on tests repeated earlier than six months will be canceled.

HOW CAN I FIND OUT WHAT SCHOOLS ACCEPT CLEP?

There are many schools that recognize CLEP as a way to earn credit. For a free booklet, <u>CLEP Test Centers and Other Participating Institutions</u>, which lists most of them, send your request, name, and address to:

> The College Board
> Box 1822
> Princeton, NJ 08541
> 800-257-9558
> or check the list at www.collegeboard.com

HOW TO USE THIS BOOK:

Recommended procedure:

1. Complete the review material. Take the short tests included at the end of the lessons.

2. If you do well on the tests, continue. If you do not, review the explanatary information.

3. After completing the review material, take the practice examination at the back of the book. When you take this sample test, try to simulate the test situation as nearly as possible:

    a. Find a quiet spot where you will not be disturbed.
    b. Time yourself accurately.
    c. Practice using the coding system

4. Correct the tests. Determine weaknesses. Go back and review those areas in which you had difficulty.

HOW THE EXAMINATIONS ARE SCORED

There is no penalty for wrong answers. Your score is computed based on the number of correct answers. When you are finished with the test make sure that every question is answered; however, you don't have to answer the question the first time you see it. If you use the coding system you will greatly increase your score.

THE CODING SYSTEM

Over the years COMEX has perfected a systematic approach to taking a multiple choice examination. This is called the coding system. It is designed to:

1. Get you through the examination as quickly as possible.

2. Have you quickly answer those questions that are easy for you.

3. Prevent time wasted on those questions that are too difficult.

4. Take advantage of all your knowledge of a particular subject. Most people think they can get credit only by knowing an answer is correct. You can also prove your knowledge by knowing an answer is incorrect. The coding system will show you how to accomplish this.

5. Get all the help possible by using the recall factor. Because you are going to read the total examination, it is possible that something in question 50 will trigger a thought that will help you answer question 3 the second time you read it.

6. Have your questions prioritized for the second reading.

HOW THE CODING SYSTEM WORKS

We are now going to make you a better test-taker, by showing all of your knowledge and using your time to the greatest advantage. Managing your time on the exam can be as important as knowing the correct answers. If you spend too much time working on difficult questions which you have no knowledge about, you might not get to some easy questions later that you would have gotten correct. This could cause a significant decrease in you score.

Let us attack some sample questions:

1. George Washington was:

    a. the father of King George Washington
    b. the father of Farah Washington
    c. the father of the Washington Laundry
    d. the father of Washington State
    e. the father of our country

As you read the questions you will eliminate all **wrong** answers:

a.	father of King George Washington	NO!
b.	father of Farah Washington	NO!
c.	father of the Washington Laundry	NO!
d.	father of Washington State	NO!
e.	the father of our country	YES. LEAVE IT ALONE.

The question now looks like this:

1.   George Washington was:

~~a.   the father of King George Washington~~
~~b.   the father of Farah Washington~~
~~c.   the father of the Washington Laundry~~
~~d.   the father of Washington State~~
e.   the father of our country

Click on the button next to the correct answer an click next.

```
00:35
              O Answer
              O Answer
              O Answer.
              O Answer
              O Answer
        |Time||Review||Mark|        |Next|
```

These are the buttons you must know how to use!

You are now finished with this question. Later when you get to the review process this question will be sorted as answered. This will be your signal to not spend any more time with this question. Any time spent will be wasted.

2.   Abraham Lincoln was responsible for:

a.   freeing the 495 freeway
b.   freeing the slaves
c.   freeing the Lincoln Memorial
d.   freeing the south for industrialization
e.   freeing the Potomac River

Go through the answers.

a.	freeing the 495 freeway	No!
b.	freeing the slaves	Maybe. Always read full question.
c.	freeing the Lincoln Memorial	No!
d.	freeing the south for industrialization	Maybe.
e.	freeing the Potomac River	No!

The question now looks like this:

2.   Abraham Lincoln was responsible for:

   a. ~~freeing the 495 freeway~~
   b. freeing the slaves
   c. ~~freeing the Lincoln Memorial~~
   d. freeing the south for industrialization
   e. ~~freeing the Potomac River~~

Should you guess? You have very good odds of getting this question correct. Pick the choice that you feel is the best answer. Often your first guess will be the best. Before clicking the next button click on the mark box. This will tell you later that you were able to eliminate 3 answers before guessing. Now click on next to go on to the next question.

3.   Franklin Roosevelt's greatest accomplishment was:

   a. building the Panama Canal
   b. solving the Great Depression
   c. putting America to work
   d. organizing the CCC Corps
   e. instituting the income tax

Go through the answers:

a. building the Panama Canal	No! That was a different Roosevelt.
b. solving the Great Depression	Maybe. Go on to the next answer.
c. putting America to work	Maybe. On to the next answer.
d. organizing the CCC Corps	Maybe. On to the next answer.
e. instituting the income tax	Maybe. Leave it alone!

The question now looks like this:

3.   Franklin Roosevelt's greatest accomplishment was:

   a. ~~building the Panama Canal~~
   b. solving the Great Depression
   c. putting America to work
   d. organizing the CCC Corps
   e. instituting the income tax

Should you answer this question now? Not yet. There might be a question later that contains information that would help you eliminate more of the answers. When you can only eliminate one answer, or none at all, your best course of action is to simply click on next. This will bring up the next question.

Now look at another question:

4.   Casper P. Phudd III was noted for:

    a.   rowing a boat
    b.   sailing a boat
    c.   building a boat
    d.   designing a boat
    e.   navigating a boat

Even if you have no idea of who Casper P. Phudd III is, read the answers:

a.	rowing a boat	I do not know.
b.	sailing a boat	I do not know.
c.	building a boat	I do not know.
d.	designing a boat	I do not know.
e.	navigating a boat	I do not know.

Since you cannot eliminate any of the answers, simply go on to the next question.

Try another question:

5.   Clarence Q. Jerkwater III

    a.   sailed the Atlantic Ocean
    b.   drained the Atlantic Ocean
    c.   flew over the Atlantic Ocean
    d.   colored the Atlantic Ocean orange
    e.   swam in the Atlantic Ocean

Even though you know nothing of Clarence Q. Jerkwater III, you read the answers.

a.	sailed the Atlantic Ocean	Possible.
b.	drained the Atlantic Ocean	No way!
c.	flew over the Atlantic Ocean	Maybe.
d.	colored the Atlantic Ocean orange	No way!
e.	swam in the Atlantic Ocean	Maybe.

The question now looks like this:

5.   Clarence Q. Jerkwater III

    a.   sailed the Atlantic Ocean
    b.   ~~drained the Atlantic Ocean~~
    c.   flew over the Atlantic Ocean
    d.   ~~colored the Atlantic Ocean orange~~
    e.   swam in the Atlantic Ocean

Do you take a guess? Not on the first reading of the answers. Let us wait to see if the recall factor will help. Do not click on an answer, but do click on mark. Then click on next to get the next question.

Continue in this manner until you finish all the questions in the section. By working in this manner you have organized the questions in a way to maximize your efficiency. When you finish with the last question click on review. This brings up the listing of all the questions. They will be listed in numerical order. This is not the way you want to view them. You sorted the questions as you went through them. You want to view the questions sorted. Click on status. Now the questions are sorted for you. Let's review what each type means:

Answered without a check mark.
You knew the correct answer.

Answered with a check mark.
You eliminated three answers.

Not answered with a check mark.
You eliminated two answers.

Not answered without a check mark.
You could not eliminate more than one answer.

The Second Time Through

Now you are ready to start your way through the test the second time. Where do you have the best chance of increasing your score? This question should always be at the top of your mind. "How do I show the testing people the maximum amount of information I know?" The best place to start is with the questions that you had some idea about, but not enough to answer. These are the questions where you could eliminate two answers. They are marked with a check mark. Clicking on review, and then status will sort the questions for you. All of the questions that are marked but have not been answered are grouped together for you.

Click on the first one in the group. Reread the question and the answers. Did anything in any of the other questions give you information to allow you to eliminate any answers? If the answer is yes that is great! The coding system has worked. If you eliminated one more answer make your guess between the remaining two. Leave the mark box checked and click on review to go back to the question list to choose your next question. What if you now know the correct answer? Mark it, and **remove** the check from the mark box. This question will now be listed as answered. You will not spend any more time on this question. Click on review to go back to your list of questions.

What should you do if you were unable to eliminate any more answers. Now you still need to guess. While your odds are not as good as if you had eliminated three answers, you will have a better chance than if you had eliminated no answers. Any time you eliminate answers before guessing means you are making an educated guess. Every educated guess you make has a higher chance of being correct than a random guess. More educated guesses means a higher score. Leave the mark box checked. This indicates that you were not sure of your answer.

Continue with this process until you finish all the questions in the group with a check mark that were not answered. Which questions should you work on next? It is now time to work on the questions you had the least knowledge about. These are the questions without a check mark that are not answered. Use the same process that you used for the previous set of questions. Can you now figure out the correct answer? If so mark it and check the box. If not eliminate as many answers as you can and then choose your best answer. If you guess make sure you check the mark box. Every time you reread a question there is a chance that it will trigger something in your memory that will help you with this question, or with one of the others.

Be very careful to keep track of time. If it is not diplayed at the top of the screen, make sure you click on the box so that it will be displayed. Do not think of the clock as your enemy. It is your friend. It keeps you on your task and keeps you moving efficiently through the test.

When you only have 5 minutes left, make sure that you have every question answered. Remember a blank space counts the same as a wrong answer. If you go through and make an educated guess at all the questions, you will get a better score than if the questions were left blank. Even if you randomly guess you should end up with one correct answer out of every five. Every correct answer will increase your score. While you are guessing, make sure you check the mark box, so that you know you guessed on that question. This allows you to review that question later if time permits.

You are now finally at the point that you only have two types of questions left, those where you knew the correct answer and those where you guessed at the answer. All of the questions are now answered. Does this mean it is time to stop? Not if you want to get your highest score. All of the questions on which you took educated guess have a check mark. Keep working on those problems. Do not waste time looking at any questions that do not have a check. You knew the correct answer and are done with them.

By using the coding system you will move quickly through the test and make sure that you see every question. It also allows you to concentrate your efforts on your strongest areas.

Practice the system while you do your exercises and tests. You can use a similar system with a piece of scratch paper. Put an "A" next to questions as you answer them. Put a check mark next to a question to refer back to it. Then use the system to go back through the test. The system is easy to master and will be an invaluable tool in your test-taking arsenal.

You have now completed the portion of the book which was designed to improve your test-taking ability. When you work the practice exercises and take the sample test, use these techniques you have just learned.

You can use the coding system on any multiple choice exam. This will not only increase your score on that test, but it will also make you more comfortable with using the system. It has been demonstrated many times that the more comfortable you are when you are taking a test the higher your score will be.

SOME BASICS FOR THE TEST DAY

1. Get to the examination location early. If you are taking the examination at a new location - check out how to get there **before** the day of the examination.

2. Choose a seat carefully.
   a. In a large room, choose a quiet corner. If possible, sit facing a wall.
   b. If you go with a friend, do not sit together.

3. Stay with your usual routine. If you normally skip breakfast, do so on the test day as well.

4. If you do not understand the proctor's directions, ask questions.

5. Do not quit. Keep going over questions you were not able to answer the first time. You may work anywhere in each section. Beat the examination, do not let it beat you!

6. If you cannot answer a question, code it and go on to the next. Do not spend a lot of time on one question unless you have already finished the rest of that section. Go through each section and do the easiest questions first, then go back to the difficult ones.

7. **Be sure** you understand the directions for **each** type of test **BEFORE you take the examination**. Not understanding the directions can cause you to lose valuable time when you are taking the actual test.

8. Remember to use the coding system.

9. If you are unfamiliar with how to use a mouse, try to get some practice. Most libraries have computers where you can practice. If you have to learn how to use the mouse at the test site you are putting yourself at a severe disadvantage.

The CLEP General Humanities Examination
Official Description of the Test

The CLEP General Examination in Humanities tests general knowledge of literature, art, and music. It is broad in its coverage, with questions on all periods from classical to contemporary and in many different fields: poetry, prose, philosophy, history of art, music, dance, and theater. The examination requires candidates to demonstrate their understanding of the humanities through recollection of specific information, comprehension and application of concepts, and analysis and interpretation of various works of art.

The test is very broad in its coverage, and it is unlikely that any one person will be well informed about all the fields it covers. The test is 90 minutes long and includes approximately 150 multiple-choice questions to be answered in two separately timed 45-minute sections.

For candidates with satisfactory scores on the Humanities examination, colleges may grant up to six semester hours (or the equivalent) of credit toward fulfillment of a distribution requirement. Some may grant credit for a particular course that matches the examination in content. Although subscores are reported for Literature and Fine Arts to indicated areas of strength and weakness, the subscores are not intended for use in awarding credit for specific courses in these areas. Subscores are computed independently of the total score; thus, an individual's total score cannot be determined by combining the two subscores. Although subscores are not designed to be used to grant course credit, colleges may require that the Fine Arts and Literature subscores be above a certain level to ensure that credit is not awarded to a student who is deficient in either of these areas.

Knowledge and Skills Required

Questions on the test require candidates to demonstrate the abilities listed below. Some questions may require more than one of the abilities.

- Knowledge of factual information (names, works, etc.) (about 50% of the examination)

- Recognition of techniques such as rhyme scheme, medium, and matters of style, and ability to identify them as characteristic of certain writers, artists, schools, or periods (about 30% of the examination)

- Understanding and interpretation of literary passages and art reproductions that are likely to be unfamiliar to most candidates (about 20 % of the examination)

The subject matter of the General Examination Humanities is drawn from the following topics.

Approximate Percent of the Examination

LITERATURE	**50%**	
DRAMA	5-10%	7-14
POETRY	15-20%	21-28
FICTION	10-15%	14-21
NONFICTION	5-10%	7-14
PHILOSOPHY	5%	7
FINE ARTS	**50%**	
VISUAL ARTS	25%	35
(PAINTING, SCULPTURE, ETC.)		
MUSIC	15%	21
PERFORMING ARTS	5%	7
ARCHITECTURE	5%	7

The test questions, drawn from the entire history of Western art and culture, are fairly evenly divided among the following periods: Classical, Medieval and Renaissance, seventeenth and eighteenth centuries, nineteenth century, and twentieth century. In addition, there are questions that draw on other cultures, such as African and Oriental. Some of the questions cross disciplines and/or chronological periods, and a substantial number test knowledge of terminology, genre, and style.

Introduction: What is "Humanities?"

During the Middle Ages, higher learning in western Europe centered on the study of the seven liberal arts: grammar, rhetoric, logic, arithmetic, astronomy, geometry and music. Later in the 1400s, some scholars rebelled against this focus of education, claiming that it overemphasized abstract subjects and values and tended to ignore humans and their values.

These scholarly rebels joined together in schools and universities of their own and proposed a new course of study; one concerned with humans instead of the spiritual and supernatural. They turned to the works of ancient Greek and Roman thinkers and writers, which they felt had given the highest, noblest, expression and study of human nature.

The key word is human. This movement called itself humanism; and, logically enough, the curriculum of its schools was dubbed humanities.

Today, the humanities are the general subjects of literature, the fine arts, music and philosophy. Some other major divisions of learning on the college level besides humanities are the social sciences (history, psychology, economics and others) and the sciences (biology, chemistry, mathematics, and so on).

The purpose of studying the humanities is to increase general knowledge and appreciation of life. It is not to teach a skill or trade. Study in the humanities develops intellectual discipline and refines one's judgment and taste. Too much emphasis on the sciences can destroy a person's sense of values by over-stressing practicality and everyday matters. To concentrate on just the practical without any attention to the humanities—and remember, that realm includes novels, books, poems, drama, movies, newspapers, television, art of every kind, music (both classical and popular)—would be, to stick with the root word, dehumanizing, not to mention boring.

We are all human, and all of us have an interest in most of the topics that together make up humanities. It is no wonder, then, that humanities is the area in which people who take the CLEP examinations score highest. You need not feel you have an insufficient background in humanities, because the things you do every day, in work and play, bring you into contact with the subject. What you need to do is organize your thinking about the subject.

This series covers literature, music and art (the three areas tested by the CLEP humanities examination). It will highlight the most important intellectual movements of each, giving some attention to representative authors and works that you will likely encounter on the CLEP examination. The purpose is not to cram you full of names and dates, just as the humanities examination is not designed to test you on specific bits of information. Instead, the idea is to broaden your cultural awareness and your understanding of the three test areas. As with the examination, the largest part of this humanities review will focus on literature, the written word. Let us begin with a literature review, specifically the topics of literary terminology, the fundamentals of poetry, and survey of great periods, works and authors. Then we will look at some fundamentals of music history and notation and finish with a survey of art.

Literature Review
Part One: Literary Terminology

In order to discuss automobiles intelligently, you have to know the language of the subject. Who can know how an engine works until they know a carburetor from a torque converter? The same is true of literature. Before you can apply yourself to understanding literature, you must know how to express yourself precisely about its parts and characteristics.

A list of the sixteen most frequently used literary terms follows. Let us look alphabetically at each term for a concise explanation and an example or two. After every group of five or so terms, you will have the opportunity to try some sample CLEP examination questions. The sample questions will tell you whether you understand the terms. If you cannot answer all the questions for each new group, more review of the terms will be in order.

ALLEGORY

An allegory is a story in which the characters (people, active objects or animals) represent abstract ideas or qualities, such as goodness, evil, love, death, lust, greed, and so on.

Allegories evoke a dual interest: one is in the events, characters and setting, the other in the ideas they are intended to convey or the significance they bear. The meaning of an allegory can be religious, social, political, satirical, or of another nature, just as long as the surface story is a logical one that conveys the characters beyond into another level of meaning, that of the idea.

Two famous allegories are **The Faerie Queene** by Spenser and Bunyan's **Pilgrim's Progress**. Spenser's is a tale of imaginary creatures and their battles, but it also brings to mind how some notions of chivalry conflict. The characters represent abstract ideas. **Pilgrim's Progress** is the story of a man trying to live a godly life. However, it is also the story of Christian people in general, who must conquer their inner obstacles to faith, such as vanity and despair.

ALLITERATION

[handwritten: B, C, D, F, G, H, J, L, M, N, P, Q, R, S, T, V, X, Z]

Alliteration is the repetition of initial consonant sounds, or any vowel sounds in successive words or syllables.

Following are some examples of alliteration. Read each one aloud, emphasizing the underlined letters or syllables.

[handwritten: VOWELS A, E, I, O, U]

EXAMPLE OF CONSONANT ALLITERATION:

• The fair breeze blew, the white foam flew,
  The furrow followed free.

EXAMPLE OF VOWEL ALLITERATION:

• Apt alliteration's artful aid is often an occasional ornament in prose.

EXAMPLE OF SYLLABIC ALLITERATION:

• The moan of doves in immemorial elms,
  And murmuring of innumerable bees.

APOSTROPHE

An **apostrophe** is the addressing of a person or thing not actually present.

This device first appeared in literature as an invocation of (or prayer to) the Muses that opened Greek poetry and epics. Subsequent writers have copied that practice. There is also a good example of apostrophe in **Romeo and Juliet**, Shakespeare's tragic play. The love-smitten Juliet is alone on her balcony when she says, "O, Romeo, Romeo! wherefore art thou Romeo?" Because she addresses a person not physically present, her action is an apostrophe.

DENOUEMENT

The **denouement** is the final unraveling of the plot in any work that tells a story.

The denouement of **Romeo and Juliet** is the double suicide of the lovers. The denouement of **Moby Dick** by Herman Melville is the death of Captain Ahab while harpooning the great, white whale.

DIDACTIC WRITING OR DIDACTICISM

Didacticism is literature whose primary aim is to expound some moral, political, or other teaching.

All literature exists to communicate something, so it is best not to classify a work as didactic unless the overriding concern is expressly moral or educational. The Latin writer Lucretius' book **De Rerum Natura** (On the Nature of Things) is a good example. It teaches the reader about the Epicurean philosophy of living. **Aesop's Fables**, which imply a lesson to be learned from the fabulous characters, are also examples of didactic writing. **Aesop's Fables** are allegories.

EPIC

An **epic** is a long narrative poem written in lofty style, presenting characters of high social position in a series of adventures. The action is tied to one central figure of heroic proportions, and the whole poem details the history of a nation or race.

Examples of some works that are classified as epics are: **The Iliad** and **The Odyssey** (both written c. 850 B.C.) by the ancient Greek poet, Homer; **The Aeneid** (c. 20 B.C.) by the Latin poet, Vergil; **Beowulf** (c. 725A.D.), an English tale of unknown authorship (epics by unknown authors are called **folk epics**); **Song of Roland** (c. 1100 A.D.), a French folk epic; **The Divine Comedy** (1321) by the Italian, Dante; and **Paradise Lost** (1667) by Milton, an Englishman.

Every epic opens with a statement of theme, an invocation of a muse to inspire and instruct the writer, and action that has already begun with no exposition (the background material follows shortly; this device is known as *in media res*, Latin for "in the middle of things"). There are catalogues of ships, rosters of armies, extensive formal speeches by the main characters and complicated language in every epic. There is also the use of elaborate comparisons, called **epic similes**. A good example of epic simile comes from John Milton's **Paradise Lost**. This is a description of a battlefield strewn with bodies:

> Angel forms, who lay entranced
> Thick as autumnal leaves that strew the brooks
> In Vallombrosa, where the Etrurian shades
> High over-arched embower; or scattered sedge
> Afloat, when with fierce winds Orion armed
> Hath vexed the Red-Sea coast, whose waves o'erthrew

Busiris and his Memphian chivalry,
While with perfidious hatred they pursued
The sojourners of Goshen, who beheld
From the safe shore their floating carcasses
And broken chariot-wheels.

HYPERBOLE

A **hyperbole** is a gross exaggeration for effect, not to be taken literally.

We use hyperbole in everyday speech to color and enliven conversation, or to make a point about something.

EXAMPLE: The expressions, "It was so hot I thought I'd sweat to death," and "There were a million ants at the picnic," are hyperboles, exaggerations to make a point.

● ●

At this point, try these sample CLEP examination questions to see how well you understand the literary terms discussed so far:

1.   In Aesop's fable "The Fox and the Grapes," the grapes allegorically represent

   (A)   fruit
   (B)   goals
   (C)   failure
   (D)   hard work
   (E)   human nature

ANSWER: The best choice is (B). In the fable, a fox spies some juicy, luscious grapes hanging from a vine in a tree. He jumps up to pluck them several times, but falls short. Rather than find another way to reach the grapes or continue trying to jump high enough, the fox says that they are probably sour, and walks away. The grapes represent goals that individuals seek, but will not work hard enough to obtain. (A) is wrong because the grapes **are** fruit—they can not represent it. Failure to reach one's goals is represented by the actions of the fox, not by the grapes, so (C) would also be incorrect, as would (D) which is also represented by the fox's actions. (E) is the subject of the whole fable.

2.   "O Romeo, Romeo! wherefore art thou Romeo?" is an example of

   (A)   alliteration
   (B)   apostrophe
   (C)   metonymy
   (D)   epic language
   (E)   hyperbole

ANSWER: (B) is the correct choice. The person being addressed is not present; therefore, the example is, by definition, apostrophe. None of the other choices could be logically correct.

4

3. Is this the face that launched a thousand ships
    And burnt the topless towers of Ilium?

    The preceding passage is an example of

    (A) hyperbole
    (B) didacticism
    (C) allegory
    (D) epic language
    (E) alliteration

ANSWER: The passage is an example of epic language: (D) is the correct choice. It is lofty in tone, and refers to a great battle. The word "Ilium" is a strong clue to those who know that the story of the battle of Ilium is the Greek epic, **The Iliad**. (A) may have been your choice because of "thousand ships" and "topless towers", but according to Homer, a thousand Greek vessels actually did sail to Ilium. "Topless towers" is exaggeration, but it is only one small phrase from the selection, not enough to make (A) the correct answer. (C) is not a logical choice. "Topless towers" is a consonant alliteration, but again only one small part of the sample. It is not enough to warrant (E) as the correct answer.

IMAGERY

Imagery is use of language to represent things, actions or ideas in a descriptive manner. Images are pictures created in the mind through words.

When an author writes about a brook, babbling and bubbling around rocks and stones, he paints a picture in our minds complete with motion and sound. Imagery is detailed literary scenery that appeals to the physical senses.

IRONY

Irony is contradiction between a situation in a story as it appears to the characters, and the truth as the audience knows it. The audience alone understands the ironic moment; the characters do not.

In his short story **The Gift of the Magi**, O. Henry creates a classic example of irony. A young married couple is poor, and neither has any worthwhile possessions except for the wife's long, flowing hair and the husband's antique, gold pocket watch. They love each other greatly, and when Christmas comes around they are sad because they have no money to buy expensive presents for each other. The woman sells her hair to a wig maker so that she can buy a gold watch chain for her husband; and the husband sells his watch to buy his wife a set of fine combs and brushes. Their actions, as only the audience sees, are ironic.

Another good example of irony occurs in the Greek play, **Oedipus Rex** by Sophocles. When a baby boy is born to King Laius of Thebes, the mystical Oracle of Delphi sends Laius a warning: that his son's fate is to grow up to kill his father and marry his mother. Fate, by definition, is unchangeable. The king, nevertheless, attempts to avoid the pre-determined events. He pins the baby's feet together and orders him to be abandoned on a mountain top to die.

However, the servant sent to carry out the deed feels pity for the infant and gives him to a shepherd from nearby Corinth. The shepherd takes him home, presenting him to be a son for the childless king and queen there. Oedipus grows up to be a strong, noble young man; but he is troubled by rumors that he is not the true son of the king and queen of Corinth. He visits the Oracle to ask the god Apollo for the truth of his parentage. The oracle replies only that his terrible fate is to kill his father and marry his mother.

Oedipus runs away from Corinth and his apparent family to try to prevent his fate from happening. While traveling, he is nearly run over by a chariot that is driven by his true father. The proud young man attacks and kills the man that he does not know is his true father.

Eventually, Oedipus wanders to Thebes, finding the city under siege by a sphinx, a beast that is half-woman, half-lion. The sphinx has vowed to kill all people she finds outside the city walls until they answer the riddle, "What animal walks on four legs in the morning, two legs in the afternoon and three legs in the evening?" Oedipus confronts the sphinx, answers correctly that man—in the morning as a baby crawling, in the afternoon as a full-grown creature walking, and in the evening as a bent, old being using a cane—walks so. He is correct. The sphinx kills herself, setting the city free; and the people, lacking a leader since the murder of their king (ironically by Oedipus, although no one, not even Oedipus, knows it), acclaim him as king. He marries his widowed mother, neither aware of the other's true identity. Tragedy comes to Oedipus later in the story when his identity is finally revealed by the shepherd who found him. Irony occurs when both Laius and Oedipus take actions to subvert their fates, because they actually bring their fates to pass.

METAPHOR

A **metaphor** is an implied comparison between two normally unrelated things, indicating a likeness or analogy between them. The objects can be identified with each other or substituted one for the other in a sentence.

One object is actually named as the other, or the normally unrelated object is used in place of an obviously appropriate word.

SOME SENTENCES CONTAINING METAPHORS:

- His room is a garbage dump. ("room" and "garbage dump" are identified with each other)
- War is hell. ("war" and "hell" are identified with each other)
- The new teacher brought order to the zoo. ("zoo" is substituted for the logically understood word, "class")

ONOMATOPOEIA

This is the use of a word whose sound suggests its meaning.

Hiss, buzz, sizzle, and slam are onomatopoetic words. Onomatopoeia also applies to whole passages of some poems and prose. An example is Edgar Allen Poe's poem *The Bells*, which in repetition of the word "bells" actually simulates the sounds of many bells ringing.

• •

Now, try some more sample CLEP examination questions about literary terms:

1. There's a certain slant of light,
   Winter Afternoons—
   That oppresses, like the Heft
   of Cathedral Tunes—

   This passage from a poem by Emily Dickinson relies heavily on the device known as

   (A) denouement
   (B) metaphor
   (C) parody
   (D) imagery
   (E) apostrophe

ANSWER: (D) is the correct choice. We can eliminate (A) because there is no story told here; therefore, there could not be any kind of climax to one. (B) is not a good choice because there are no indirect comparisons; in fact, the only comparison is in lines three and four, and it is a direct comparison using the word "like". That is called a **simile**—more on that term later. (C) would not be a logical selection because there is no well-known work being made fun of in the passage. (E) would be wrong since no one except the reader is addressed.

2. So fierce you whirr and pound you drums—
   so shrill you bugles blow.

   "Whirr" and "pound" from this passage...

   (A) are onomatopoetic
   (B) indicate epic simile
   (C) describe metaphorically
   (D) represent didacticism
   (E) are alliterative

ANSWER: (A) is the correct choice, because the words suggest their meaning with the sound they make. "Whirr" and "pound" actually mock the sound that drums make. No lofty comparisons are made in the passage, so (B) would be incorrect. In fact, no comparisons at all are made in this descriptive sample, so (C) is also incorrect. There is no overriding concern for teaching here, thus (D) is wrong. "Bugles blow" is the only alliterative phrase in the sample; "whirr" and "pound" do not involve the repetition of consonants, vowels, or syllable, therefore (E) is also logically incorrect.

3. On beachy slush and sand spirits of snow fierce slanting.

   The line above illustrates Walt Whitman's use of

   (A) irony
   (B) imagery
   (C) alliteration
   (D) allegory
   (E) denouement

ANSWER: The repetition of the consonant sound "s" runs throughout the passage in the words slush, sand, spirits, snow, fierce and slanting. This is alliteration pure and simple; (C) is the correct answer. (A) is not a logical choice because no contradicting situation is presented. There is not enough of a story for anyone to say it is (D) or (E). A case might be made for (B) as a possible answer since there is description of a scene involved. However, the evidence to alliteration is greater. The best choice is (C).

PERSONIFICATION

Personification is a figure of speech that gives human traits (thought, action, feeling) to animals, objects or ideas.

The story of Goldilocks and the three bears personifies the bears by giving them human characteristics of speech and life in a house. Whoever heard a baby bear say, "My porridge is too hot!"? George Orwell's book, **Animal Farm** is replete with personification of a farm full of animals who overthrow their cruel human master and set up a government.

HERE ARE SOME MORE PERSONIFICATIONS:

* The storm lashed the naked, helpless shore. ("Storm", given the ability to whip, and "shore", given the trait of being unclothed, personified)

* Time's cruel hand snatched her away from him. ("Time", a concept, is personified with emotion and a hand)

SATIRE

Satire is a form of writing that blends criticism with humor and wit, ridiculing a person or an institution with the purpose of inspiring reform.

Popular satire today is found in **MAD Magazine** and **National Lampoon**. They make fun of people, social practices, movies, commercials, politicians, television, and so on, with the motive of revealing their flaws.

Satirists have written since the Greek playwright Aristophanes (c. 400 B.C.). The Latin authors Horace (60 B.C.) and Juvenal (c. 60 A.D.) wrote satirical poems. Alexander Pope and Jonathan Swift were famous English satirists of the 18th century.

SIMILE

A **simile** is a direct comparison between two unlike things, using connectives such as "like" and "as."

In the sentence, "John swims like a fish," the grace and natural ability with which John swims are compared with the grace and natural ability with which a fish swims. Such a comparison is a simile. As with metaphor, two unlike things are compared in a simile (in this case, John and a fish). The key to knowing the difference between simile and metaphor is the use or absence of the words "like", "as" or other directly comparing words. A simile always has the comparing words; a metaphor does not.

SOME OTHER SIMILES:

* He eats like a horse. (A "horse" and a "man" are directly compared, introduced by the word "like".)

- That building is as tall as a mountain. (A "building" and a "mountain," again two unlike things, are directly compared. The comparison is introduced by "as.")

SYMBOLISM

Symbolism is the use of an object to represent another object or idea. It sees the immediate, unique and personal emotional response as the proper subject of art. Symbols are used by authors to recreate in their readers the feelings or truths that are impossible to communicate verbally.

If you were to drive an unfamiliar road and to come across an octagon nailed to a post at an intersection, you would probably stop your car. That is because the octagon has become a symbol for the concept "stop." When a driver encounters an octagon along a roadside, it communicates the message to him that, for his own safety, he must stop his vehicle and check traffic. In an elementary way, that is how symbolism in literature functions.

When people see a cross atop a steeple, printed on a book cover or carved in stone over a grave, it communicates a message to them. The message is that the building, book, or grave has some Christian meaning or purpose. While the stop sign is denotative in its meaning (it spells out a precise message), the cross is connotative (it brings to mind many different messages). It can serve as a welcome to some, as a reminder of hope and goodness to others. Still others might see a cross as nothing more than the trademark of a social movement. Now we are getting close to the operation of symbolism in literature.

Authors use characters, animals, things, actions and descriptions to represent emotions or truths that can not be communicated properly by definition. In Herman Melville's novel, **Moby Dick**, a great white whale symbolizes evil. A flowing river is a popular symbol for life, or the passage of time in life, in several of the world's great literary works.

Symbols can be recognized and identified as such; but the meanings they convey, in the purest sense, can only be felt. We may attempt to describe them and analyze them, but they must be felt in order to understand their full meaning.

THEME

The theme is the central or dominating idea of a work (this includes movies, paintings and all works of art). It may be spelled out by the work or sometimes must be understood from it. Themes are always expressed in terms of all mankind and the universe.

All works of art—be they books, magazine articles, scholarly papers, statues, paintings, even buildings—have themes. The theme of much of Walt Whitman's poetry is that man is innately a good creature. The romantic English poet William Wordsworth carried the same theme further. His works tell us that in natural surroundings a man is a good being, but also one corrupted by city life.

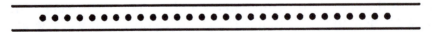

Once more, try a few sample CLEP examination questions to test your understanding of these literary terms:

1. The saying "as blind as a bat" is a

   (A) metaphor
   (B) symbolism
   (C) colloquialism
   (D) simile
   (E) didacticism

ANSWER: (D) is the best choice. "as blind as a bat" is a direct comparison between some understood object not named (probably a person) and a bat. The words "as ...as" introduce the comparison. Metaphor requires indirect comparison by identifying or substituting a normally unrelated thing with another, thus (A) is incorrect. (C), which means a locally used expression with no meaning for people of another region, is not correct, because "blind as a bat" is used and understood in most places where English is spoken. There is no overriding concern for teaching, so (E) is wrong.

2. Two or three days and nights went by; I reckon they swum by, they slid along so quiet and smooth and lovely.

   The passage above demonstrates a writer's use of

   (A) personification
   (B) imagery
   (C) alliteration
   (D) metaphor
   (E) epic language

ANSWER: Personification, (A), is the best choice. Days, which are really nothing more than concepts, are given human features when the author says that "they swum by" and "they slid along." Because we could never actually see a day "swimming by," we know that (B) is incorrect; the author appeals to our humor and does not try to paint a physical picture that appeals to our physical senses through our imaginations. There is no repetition of initial consonants, vowel sounds, or syllables, thus (C) would be an illogical selection. There is no comparison in which the days are identified or substituted with another thing (such as, "the days were fish—they swum by"); therefore, (D) is wrong. Finally, the language in the passage is, while effective, uneducated, poor English. Epics are written in lofty style, so the passage could not be an example of epic language (E).

3. How weary, stale, flat and unprofitable
   Seem to me all the uses of this world!
   Fie on't, ah, fie, 'tis an unweeded garden
   That grows to seed.

   The comparison of the earth and garden in this passage from Shakespeare's play, **Hamlet**, is

   (A) didactic
   (B) simile
   (C) metaphor
   (D) personification
   (E) onomatopoeia

ANSWER: It is an indirect comparison in which the earth and an unweeded garden are identified with each other, without the signal words like and as. Thus, the correct answer is (C). (B) is a comparison, but a direct one used with the signal words, and it is not the answer. **Hamlet** has no overriding purpose to teach, no obvious moral, so (A) would be an illogical choice. The world is given the characteristics of an unweeded garden, a thing. Personification means attributing human characteristics to something, so (D) can not be the correct answer. There is nothing lofty about the passage; (E) would be a poor choice.

Now you have had a look at the meanings of sixteen important literary terms, the terms students are most likely to encounter on the CLEP humanities examination. After studying this section, you should have a good grasp of the "shop talk" of literature. Use the sample CLEP questions to determine if your understanding of the terms is sufficient. Do not attempt to review any more CLEP humanities material until you have mastered this first lesson. Finally, until the test day, look for and name examples of these literary terms in your everyday reading and conversation.

Literature Review
Part Two: Some Fundamentals of Poetry

Because most early literature and many other important works are written in verse, you need an understanding of the structure of verse to be able to answer questions about them. The CLEP Humanities examination contains many questions that directly or indirectly involve the technical aspects of poetry. Although the topic is not difficult, its unusual terms can be baffling to the beginner and confusing to students who have previously studied it.

METER AND FOOT

The structure of poetry is almost arithmetical when analyzed. Two elements are involved in the writing and reading of poetry: meter and foot.

Meter is the repeating pattern of stressed and unstressed syllables established in a line of poetry. The stressed syllable is also called the accented or "long" syllable, and it is marked in a line of poetry with an accent mark (′). The unstressed syllable is known as the unaccented or "short" syllable, and is marked with a cap-like symbol (∪).

Foot is one unit of meter in poetry. Each unit of the repeated pattern in a line may be counted, and the length of the line is expressed by the number of feet. A foot can have two or three syllables, generally one stressed syllable and one or more unstressed syllables. A line of poetry may have one, two or as many feet as possible, but it is rare to find one with more than eight feet.

Poetic feet are named by the arrangement of stressed and unstressed syllables in the foot. The basic types are:

Name of Foot	Repeating Meter of Foot
iambic	short-long
trochaic	long-short
anapestic	short-short-long
dactylic	long-short-short
spondaic	long-long
pyrrhic	short-short

Following is an explanation of each type of metrical foot. An example from actual poetry will be given for each. It will be marked for long and short syllables to illustrate the repeating pattern for you. Read the example lines aloud; exaggerate the long and short syllables so that you can hear the pattern.

1. **IAMB**—the iambic foot is a two-syllable foot with the stress on the second syllable. This is the most common foot in English language poetry. The repeating pattern is **short syllable-long syllable**.

EXAMPLE: ⏑ ´ ⏑ ´ ⏑ ´ ⏑ ´ ⏑ ´
A book of verses underneath the bough,

⏑ ´ ⏑ ´ ⏑ ´ ⏑ ´ ⏑ ´
A jug of wine, a loaf of bread—and thou.

— Edward Fitzgerald,
The Rubaiyat of Omar Khayyam

2. **TROCHEE**—the trochaic foot consists of a stressed syllable followed by an unstressed syllable. The repeating pattern is **long-short**, just the opposite of the iamb.

EXAMPLE: ´ ⏑ ´ ⏑ ´ ⏑ ´ ⏑
Double, double, toil and trouble,

´ ⏑ ´ ⏑ ´ ⏑ ´ ⏑
Fire burn and cauldron bubble.

— William Shakespeare, ***Macbeth***

3. **ANAPEST**—the anapestic foot consists of three syllables with the stress on the last syllable. The repeating pattern in the line is **short-short-long**.

EXAMPLE: ⏑ ⏑ ´ ⏑ ⏑ ´ ⏑ ⏑ ´ ⏑ ⏑
With the sheep in the fold and the cows in their stalls.

4. **DACTYL**—the dactylic foot contains three syllables with the stress on the first syllable. It is the reverse of the anapest. The dactylic pattern is **long-short-short**.

EXAMPLE: ´ ⏑ ⏑ ´ ⏑ ⏑ ´ ⏑ ⏑ ´ ⏑ ⏑
Love again, song again, nest again, young again.

5. **SPONDEE**—the spondaic foot consists of two stressed syllables. Compound words are examples of spondees. Spondees are normally mixed in with other types of metrical feet in a line for variation. The repeating pattern is **long-long**.

EXAMPLE: ´ ´   ´ ´   ´ ´
heartbreak   childhood   football

6. **PYRRHIC**—the pyrrhic foot contains two unstressed syllables. This type of foot is rare. Like the spondee, it is interspersed in lines of poetry with other types of metrical feet for variation. It is difficult and pointless to give examples of pyrrhic feet from poetry; you will know them when you find them if you remember that they differ from the prevailing pattern, and that they are two successive short syllables.

LINES

Now that you know the kinds of individual metrical feet and their proper names, we can concentrate on describing an entire line of poetry.

When we count the total number of feet in a line, we can give them a name that describes the length of the line. The basic kinds of lines are named by the number of feet in each:

Name of Line	Number of Feet
monometer	one-foot line
dimeter	two-foot line
trimeter	three-foot line
tetrameter	four-foot line
pentameter	five-foot line
hexameter	six-foot line
heptameter	seven-foot line
octometer	eight-foot line

Let us look at several of the examples previously used for illustrating types of metrical feet, and name the length of each line. Remember, first determine the pattern of stressed and unstressed syllables in the line of poetry; then and only then count the number of units of the pattern in each line to name its length.

EXAMPLE: Here again is the selection from ***The Rubaiyat of Omar Khayyam***. It is iambic poetry. The repeating pattern is short-long:

    ∪ ′ ∪ ′ ∪ ′ ∪ ′ ∪ ′
A book of verses underneath the bough,

    ∪ ′ ∪ ′ ∪ ′ ∪ ′ ∪ ′
A jug of wine, a loaf of bread—and thou.

Now in your book draw a slash (/) after the last syllable in each foot (you need not draw a slash at the end of a line). The lines above should now look like this:

    ∪ ′ ∪ ′ ∪ ′ ∪ ′ ∪ ′
A book / of ver / ses un / derneath / the bough,

    ∪ ′ ∪ ′ ∪ ′ ∪ ′ ∪ ′
A jug / of wine, / a loaf / of bread / —and thou.

Count the number of iambic feet, or units of iambic pattern, that you have made with the slashes. There are five: a five-foot line is called pentameter.

EXAMPLE: Try again with the example from Shakespeare's ***Macbeth***. Remember "Double, double, toil and trouble"? Here it is properly accented. Draw slashes after each trochaic foot:

    ′ ∪ ′ ∪ ′ ∪ ′ ∪
Double, double, toil and trouble,

    ′ ∪ ′ ∪ ′ ∪ ′ ∪
Fire burn and cauldron bubble.

It should now look like this:

    ′ ∪ ′ ∪ ′ ∪ ′ ∪
Double, / double, / toil and / trouble,

    ′ ∪ ′ ∪ ′ ∪ ′ ∪
Fire / burn and / cauldron / bubble.

Count the number of feet in each line. There are four: a four-foot line is called tetrameter. It is simple, once you are familiar with the words and the process.

By combining type of feet with length of lines, we create two-word names that instantly describe the stress of syllables and the number of feet in each line. Thus, the lines from **The Rubaiyat of Omar Khayyam** are written in a form called iambic pentameter. The lines from **Macbeth** are written in trochaic tetrameter.

●●●●●●●●●●●●●●●●●●●●●●●●●●●●●●●

At this point try some sample CLEP examination questions about the fundamentals of poetry to test your understanding of how to analyze poetry. If you do not get all of them correct, review this section again.

1. Whose woods these are I think I know.
    His house is in the village though;
    He will not see me stopping here
    To watch his woods fill up with snow.

    These lines from Frost's **"Stopping by Woods on a Snowy Evening"** are

    (A) trochaic
    (B) iambic
    (C) spondaic
    (D) plain verse
    (E) pyrrhic

ANSWER: The repeated pattern of stressed and unstressed syllables is short-long:

$$\cup \quad ' \quad \cup \quad ' \cup \quad ' \cup \quad '$$
Whose woods these are I think I know.

Such poetry is iambic, and (B) is the correct answer. None of the others is a logical choice.

2. Green pastures she views in the midst of the dale,
    Down which she so often has tripped with her pail;
    And a single small cottage, a nest like a dove's;
    The one only dwelling on earth that she loves.

    These lines by William Wordsworth are written in

    (A) iambic tetrameter
    (B) iambic pentameter
    (C) anapestic tetrameter
    (D) dactylic pentameter
    (E) dactylic tetrameter

ANSWER: By going through the first two lines, marking long and short syllables, we find that the dominant metrical foot is anapestic. Note that although an iambic foot opens each line it does not change the way we name the line. Consider the iamb an incomplete anapest instead. **Always name the line by the dominant meter.** By counting the number of anapestic feet, which you should have marked by slashes:

$$\cup \quad ' \quad \cup \quad \cup \quad ' \quad \cup \quad \cup \quad ' \quad \cup \quad \cup \quad '$$
Green pas / tures she views / in the midst / of the dale

15

we find that there are four feet to a line. The length of metrical line is tetrameter. Put the two together—anapestic tetrameter—and the answer is (C). Usually, marking two lines for stress patterns and feet in a question of this type is sufficient for determining the answer. However, if you are unsure of the structure, continue marking the lines in the sample selection until the answer becomes obvious to you. Never read possible answers and try to fit one to the question; always analyze the poetic sample when you are asked to identify the structure and then look for the choice that is correct. Do not hesitate to mark your test book when you take the CLEP examination, just as you have marked your review text here. It is perfectly allowable and beneficial for you to do so.

3. Workers earn it,
    Spendthrifts burn it,
    Bankers lend it,
    Women spend it,
    Forgers fake it,
    I could use it.

The poem quoted above is written in

(A) trochaic dimeter
(B   iambic pentameter
(C) trochaic tetrameter
(D) iambic dimeter
(E) iambic trimeter

ANSWER: After marking the first few lines for stressed and unstressed syllables:

′ ∪ ′ ∪   ′ ∪   ′ ∪
Workers earn it, Spendthrifts burn it

you should have found that they are trochaic. After adding slash marks between trochaic feet and counting the number in each line, you should have found them to be two-foot lines, dimeter. The correct answer is (A) trochaic dimeter. No other answer could be correct.

If you were unable to answer all three questions correctly, go back and review the preceding section.

RHYME

Beyond the breakdown of poetry into rhythms, as in types of feet and length of lines, there is a final consideration: rhyme. Rhyme also has technical names you should be familiar with in preparing for the CLEP humanities examination.

Poetry means rhyme to many people, as it probably meant to ancient societies before writing was invented. Scholars theorize that ancient peoples memorized stories and passed them down from generation to generation (this is known as **oral tradition**). Rhyme, it is thought, helped them remember. It is no wonder then, that the earliest words of literature were written with regular rhythm and definite rhyme. Later writers, venerating the original style of ancients such as the Greek epic poet Homer, copied their poetic style for works they deemed to be of highest significance. Even today, poetry—often rhyming, although not necessarily—has been regarded as the noblest literary expression.

Rhyme is described, generally, by three kinds of **verse forms**:

1. **RHYMED VERSE** is poetry that rhymes at the end of lines.

2. **BLANK VERSE** is poetry written in iambic pentameter without end rhyme. Shakespeare's works and all epics in English use this form.

3. **FREE VERSE** consists of lines that do not have a regular meter and do not rhyme.

Rhyme in a poem can be diagrammed by assigning consecutive letters for each new end sound.

EXAMPLE: One would diagram Shelley's **"To Wordsworth"** in this manner:

Poet of Nature, thou has wept to know		a
That things depart which never may return:		b
Childhood and youth, friendship and love's first glow,		a
Have fled like sweet dreams, leaving thee to mourn.		b
These common woes I feel. One loss is mine	5	c
Which thou too feel'st, yet I alone deplore.		d
Thou wert as a lone star, whose light did shine		c
On some frail bark in winter's midnight roar:		d
Thou hast like to a rock-built refuge stood		e
Above the blind and battling multitude:	10	e
In honoured poverty thy voice did weave		f
Songs consecrate to truth and liberty,—		g
Deserting these, thou leavest me to grieve,		f
Thus, having been, that thou shouldst cease to be.		g

The **rhyme scheme**, or diagrammed rhyme, of **"To Wordsworth"** is described as a-b-a-b-c-d-c-d-e-e-f-g-f-g. Imperfect rhymes, such as "return" and "mourn" in lines 2 and 4 and "stood" and "multitude" in lines 9 and 10, do count in the rhyme scheme and receive the same letter designation.

● ●

Once again, try some sample CLEP questions to measure your comprehension of these principles of poetry.

1.   Now cracks a noble heart. Good night, sweet prince,
       And flights of angels sing thee to thy rest.

       The preceding lines from William Shakespeare's *Hamlet* are an example of

       (A)   epic language
       (B)   blank verse
       (C)   heroic couplet
       (D)   an alexandrine
       (E)   terza rima

ANSWER: Because these lines are written in iambic pentameter without end rhyme, we know they are blank verse. Shakespeare wrote all of his plays in this style, and that is another hint that (B) is the correct answer. While the language is lofty and moving, it does not involve elaborate comparisons that signify epic language, so (A) is not the correct answer. **Heroic couplet** is rhyming iambic pentameter but these lines do not rhyme and (C) is incorrect. **Alexandrine** (D) is iambic hexameter and is an incorrect choice. **Terza rima** is a three-line stanza in iambic pentameter with interwoven rhyme scheme (a-b-a, b-c-b and so on). The example is unrhymed and consists of only two lines, so (E) is obviously incorrect.

2. Be her eternal throne
   Built in our hearts alone—
       God save the Queen!
   Let the oppressor hold
   Canopied seats of gold;
   She sits enthroned of old
       O'er our hearts Queen.

   The rhyme scheme of this verse from Shelley's **"A New National Anthem"** could be described as

   (A)   a-a-b-b-c-c-d
   (B)   a-b-a-b-c-d-d
   (C)   a-b-a-c-d-c-d
   (D)   a-a-b-c-c-c-b
   (E)   a-b-c-d-a-b-d

ANSWER: The correct answer is (D).

18

Literature Review
Part Three: Major Authors and Works

Students will find it useful to review the major literary movements, and the authors and works associated with them before taking the CLEP Humanities examination. In many cases, you will already be familiar with them and the review will bring to mind things previously learned. In other cases, this chapter will serve as a concise guide to understanding their significance. As in the first two parts of the Literature Review, sample questions are interspersed among the material. The questions have been specifically designed to measure your understanding, while familiarizing you with the test-taking process.

ANCIENT GREEK LITERATURE

The oldest written record of Greece, and the earliest work of literary importance, is **The Iliad**. Written around 1,000 B.C., the long, narrative poem contains stories of a civilized people from whom modern society descends intellectually, artistically and politically. **The Iliad** and other ancient works tell stories considered half-story, half-legend, and detail the Greek religion.

The Greeks made their gods the physical superiors of humans in human form, but only moral equals. Thus Mount Olympus, home of the gods, was similar in many ways to life on earth. Each god had a position in the heavenly hierarchy and served as patron god of some earthly characteristic.

NAME OF GOD		DOMAIN
GREEK NAME	**ROMAN NAME**	
Zeus (king of the gods)	Jupiter	rain; clouds; thunderbolts
Hera (queen of the gods)	Juno	marriage; married women
Poseidon	Neptune	the sea
Hades	Pluto	underworld; wealth
Phoebus Apollo	Apollo	sun; light; truth; healing
Aphrodite	Venus	love, beauty
Pallas Athena	Minerva	wisdom
Ares	Mars	war
Artemis	Diana	wildlife
The Muses		inspiration for literature, science and the arts
Hermes	Mercury	commerce; Zeus' messenger
Dionysus	Bacchus	wine; theatre

The Iliad is the story of the great war between the united armies of Greece and the powerful city-state of Troy. Although the epic poem itself does not give any, the background of the Trojan War has been pieced together from other Greek literature. The conflict was grounded in a dispute among three goddesses: Aphrodite, Hera and Pallas Athena.

At a heavenly wedding on Olympus, the goddess of discord (Eris) plotted trouble because she was not invited. She tossed a golden apple engraved "For the Fairest" into the hall. All the goddesses wanted it; but Aphrodite, Hera and Pallas Athena were chosen by the crowd to be finalists. The three asked Zeus to select the winner, but he wisely declined. Instead, he sent them to Mount Ida near Troy to find the young Trojan prince, Paris, who, because of his fine eye for beauty, would decide.

King Priam of Troy had been told by the Oracle of Delphi that Paris, would someday be the ruin of his nation; so he kept Paris out in the countryside shepherding as much as possible. Despite the remote location, the three goddesses found Paris; but rather than ask him directly to pick the most beautiful, each tried to bribe him for the awarding of the golden apple. Hera offered to make him the lord of Europe and Asia. Pallas Athena promised to make him leader of a Trojan force that would conquer arch-enemy Greece. Aphrodite said that the fairest woman in the world would be his. He awarded the apple to Aphrodite.

The goddess of love transported Paris to the home of Menelaus, King of Sparta, in Greece. Menelaus was married to Helen, the woman acknowledged most beautiful in the land. All the great men of Greece had courted Helen as a maiden, but did so under an agreement with her father that all would defend and aid her eventually selected husband. Thus, when Paris came and carried Helen off, the entire Greek nation was obligated to fight Troy.

The greatest Greek warriors were called to join the great attack on Troy; but two, Odysseus and Achilles, tried to stay out of the fight. Odysseus knew the strife that he and his family would suffer as a result of the war and feigned madness by plowing his fields and sowing salt. The ruse failed, however. To keep his honor, Odysseus was forced to go. Achilles was the son of Peleus and Thetis, a sea nymph. Thetis sought to make her baby son immortal by dipping him in the underworld river, Styx. Thetis failed to dip the part by which she held Achilles, his heel, and left him vulnerable in that one spot. The mother knew Achilles fate was to die on the battlefield of Troy. She sought to keep the now strong, young man out of the war by sending him away dressed as a girl. But Odysseus, dispatched to find him, discovered the trick and took Achilles with him to the port city Aulis, where one thousand Greek ships full of soldiers set sail for Troy.

The war lasted ten years and divided the gods. They fought with each other and for their favorite sides. Pallas Athena, Poseidon and Hera worked for the Greeks while Aphrodite, Ares, Apollo, and Artemis aided the Trojans. Hector and Aeneas led the Trojan forces of King Priam. Achilles, Ajax, and Odysseus were the great warriors of General Agamemnon's Greek army. When Achilles and Hector met head on, the Greek was victorious and sealed the eventual doom of Troy. Just moments after Achilles' triumph, though, Paris, the young man who started it all, felled Achilles with an arrow to the heel.

The Odyssey is the story of Odysseus' wanderings and misfortunes as he tried to make his way home to Greece from conquered Troy. Angered gods, aroused by the desecration of sanctuaries by the victorious Greek soldiers, caused great storms to blow ships off course and sink many of them. Frequently shipwrecked, he traveled to the land of the Lotus Eaters and the island of the Cyclops named Polyphemus. He sailed the enchanted straits of Scylla and Charybdis, and passed the island of the beautiful singing cannibals, the Sirens. He also had many other adventures. The tales of **The Odyssey** further enlighten us about the Greek mind, the early Mediterranean world and mythology.

After ten more years of wandering, Odysseus returned to his kingdom of Ithaca and found his wife besieged by suitors seeking to marry the presumed widow for her wealth. With the help of a servant, Odysseus, the great warrior and king who had survived the Trojan War and all the adventures of the world, cleared the suitors and renewed his life.

Drama was a much-prized entertainment in Ancient Greece, and the oldest of the Greek master dramatists remains today one of literature's greatest writers of tragedy. **Aeschylus** (524-456 B.C.) served as a soldier in the army which at the Battle of Marathon, repelled Persia's invasion of Europe. He was austere, reason-ruled, a conservative aristocrat, and humble: he once described his plays as "crumbs gathered from Homer's banquet." His concerns were ethical problems, guilt, hereditary evil, and divine justice. Grand themes such as these are difficult to tackle in single plays; Aeschylus wrote mostly trilogies. Trilogies are three plays that follow in sequence and share some characters. They were all performed, with short breaks between, on the same day in Ancient Greece. Out of 72 plays Aeschylus wrote, seven are extant (that is, surviving today):

- **Prometheus Bound**, the story of creation and the rise of Zeus to king of heaven

- **The Persians and the Suppliants**, are plays honoring Greek military victories

- **The Seven Against Thebes**

- **Agamemnon, The Libation Pourers** and **The Furies**, together know as **The Orestia Trilogy**. In **Agamemnon**, heroic figures very much like Homer's are caught up in acts of hereditary evil set into motion by murder. Agamemnon, you will remember from **The Iliad**, was general in command of the Greek forces against Troy. He was faced with a problem when the country's men assembled at Aulis to sail to war. The winds blew continuously from the east, preventing the army from sailing to Troy. After a month of unfavorable breezes, Agamemnon knew the gods were causing the delay and he went to the Oracle of Delphi to learn the cause. One of his soldiers had killed a hare on the way to Aulis, angering the goddess Diana. She would allow the winds to change only if the commander-in-chief would sacrifice his daughter, Iphigenia. Although heart-rent, Agamemnon was ruled by his ambition to conquer Troy and exalt Greece and himself, so he did. The winds changed and the Greeks sailed on to eventual victory. During the ten years of war, Clytemnestra, his wife, mourned Iphigenia's death and plotted to avenge the murder. Upon Agamemnon's triumphant return, she lured him to bed, where she stabbed him. In **The Libation Pourers**, the other children of the general avenge him by killing their mother. In **The Furies,** a son, Orestes, atones for his killing of Clytemnestra and ends the blood feud in his family.

Sophocles (497-406 B.C.) lived during the Golden Age of Greece. At the young age of 28 he defeated Aeschylus in the annual Athenian drama competition. His plays portray the capacity for human error in actions and judgment, the depravity of evil and man's limitless suffering for it. Among his plays are:

- **Ajax**, the story of the humiliation and suicide of Greece's great warrior at Troy

- **Electra**, about fruitless vengeance

- **Antigone**, a triple suicide resulting from lack of reason and corruption

- **Oedipus the King**, a play of patricide, incest and suicide

In all his plays, Sophocles' frequently recurring theme is any person's fruitless fight against fate.

Euripides (480-406 B.C.) wrote about ethics, politics, pacifism, and the conflicts caused when leaders attempt to be rational and humanitarian. Among his great works are:

- *Medea*
- *Electra*
- *Hecuba*
- *Hippolytus*
- *Iphigenia at Aulis*
- *The Trojan Women*, detailing the tragedy of war through the example of the fall of Troy. Acting inhumanely, the Greeks kill all the children of Troy so that the race can never again rise. Tragically portrayed are the murder of the Trojan champion Hector's daughter and the throwing of his baby son, the last child, from the top of the battlements. With this last death, Troy's final sacrifice is accomplished and the world's once-greatest city-state is extinct.

LATIN LITERATURE

While the Romans were the Greek's military superiors, they were generally not as culturally innovative. The residents of the Italian peninsula copied Greek architecture, art and literature. They even adopted Greek religion, changing the names of the gods to give them a Roman identity. (See the chart of the Greek and Roman gods on page 19.)

Everything in the Roman world was written in Latin. We call Roman writings Latin literature.

Vergil (70-19 B.C.) was the greatest Latin author, and he wrote an epic called **The Aeneid**. It was written when Augustus, known as Octavian during his pre-emperor days, gained absolute power in the Roman Empire by crushing the armies of Marcus Antonius and Cleopatra. He ruled with an iron hand, restored order to the empire, and established a long period of peace called the **Pax Augusta**. All those things fired Vergil's generation with enthusiasm for the stable new Roman order. Augustus commissioned Vergil to write an epic poem that would exalt the empire, create a founder of the race that the emperor felt would soon rule the world, and make Augustus a descendant of the gods.

Part one of **The Aeneid** traces the Roman ancestry to Troy, specifically to the warrior Aeneas. You will recall from **The Iliad,** he was second-greatest only to Hector in the Trojan camp. According to Homer's account, Aeneas was the son of Aphrodite (Venus in the Roman version). A demigod, he could meet Augustus' requirements for a founder of the Roman race. The story says that when the Greeks captured Troy, Aeneas escaped with his parents and little son and sailed away to seek a new home. After long wanderings reminiscent of Odysseus (Ulysses in Latin) and many tribulations on land and sea, he and his band of Trojans reached Italy. Aeneas' voyage took him to Crete (where he learned his divine destiny), Sicily, and Carthage (home of Queen Dido, who waylaid the Roman hero for many months with her love) before the landing on the Italian west coast.

The visit of the Roman founder to the underworld makes up part two of **the Aeneid**. At the advice of his mother, Venus, Aeneas sought out a creature called the Sibyl, who could tell his fortune and guide him to the underworld. There Aeneas could ask advice on life and power from his dead father, King Priam.

Part three concentrates on the arrival of Aeneas and the Trojan remnant at the west coast of the Italian peninsula. There was little opposition to the group's setting up to live there until the goddess Juno stirred up local tribes of the Rutulians and the Etruscans against him. The Trojans fled up the Tiber River to the home of Evander, a friendly tribal king; upon that spot Rome would someday be established. Evander arranged allies for the Trojans from the enemies of the powerful, greedy Rutulian warrior and king, Turnus. An epic battle for the control of the peninsula began, but it ground to a stalemate. The two sides knew that the winner of a face-to-face fight between Aeneas and Turnus would be the ruler of the land. A battle of superhuman proportions finally occurred and Aeneas won.

Vergil's poem ends with Turnus' death. Aeneas, we are to assume, went on to marry a local princess and found the Roman race—who, Vergil says, "left to other nations such things as art and science, and ever remembered that they were destined to bring under their empire the peoples of earth, to impose the rule of submissive nonresistance, to spare the humble and to crush the proud."

Plautus (254-184 B.C.) and **Terence** (195-159 B.C.) were the best Latin playwrights. They borrowed the plots of Menander, a Greek writer of dramatic comedy, but added elements of style that sharpened the verbal wit of the characters. Letter-writing, the best by **Cicero** (106-43 B.C.), and satire, especially that of **Horace** (65-8 B.C.) and **Juvenal** (A.D. 60-131), were also honored as literary forms by Latin authors.

THE MIDDLE AGES

The period between the fall of the Roman Empire in A.D. 476 and the last of the Crusades in the 1300s is known as the Middle Ages. Learning was largely confined to the church—few people knew how to write, fewer still practiced the art. The literature created during the medieval period was largely drama. Plays about the wonders of the Bible, known as **mystery** or **miracle plays**, evolved from scripture readings. Priests began using dialogue to enliven the reading of the lessons in church. One-act plays performed in front of the altar, then full-blown dramas performed outside on the steps of cathedrals evolved. The most noteworthy ones are:

- *Abraham and Isaac*

- *The Second Shepherd's Play*

- *Everyman*, an allegory as the list of characters for the play reveals (Everyman, Death, Fellowship, Kindred, Goods, Good-Deeds, Strength, Discretion, Five Wits, Beauty, Knowledge, Confession, Angel and, of course, God). It is not hard to connect the characters who perform the physical action of the play with the abstract ideas they represent. *Everyman* portrays the basic struggles of humans in life, who are pure as children, corrupted as they age, and ultimately forgiven.

With the fall of the Greek and Roman world civilizations, one might suspect that the great epic form of writing died. Surprisingly, it continued into the Middle Ages.

Beowulf, an epic poem written in Old English around 700-800, is one of the most important pieces of Anglo-Saxon literature of the period. Written in poetic form, it is the story of a young warrior with "the strength of thirty men" who leads a company of his earls, or tribesmen, to Denmark from England to kill the monster Grendel. The hero also slays Grendel's ferocious mother, and a dragon. Beowulf dies, however, from wounds received in battle with the dragon. The poem demonstrates the qualities revered by Anglo-Saxons: loyalty, courage, strength and generosity.

Other epics were written in the Middle Ages, most notable among them *The Divine Comedy* by **Dante Alighieri**, an Italian who lived from 1265 to 1321. Written in three parts, *The Divine Comedy* details the author's journey through Hell, Purgatory and Heaven, guided by an angel. The descent through Hell, the subject of *Inferno*, is probably the best known and most widely read of the three books of *The Divine Comedy*. It describes how the angel leads Dante through a gate near a cave. The portal is inscribed, "Abandon hope all ye who enter here." The medieval notion of Hell held that those condemned spent eternity there, and Dante outlines to the tiniest degree the many different levels and rooms in which a thousand eternal punishments were carried out. The punishments increased (as did the depth into earth) with the magnitude of the sin. At the bottom of Hell, he says, was Judas, who betrayed Christ.

The extensive tour of the lower world ends when the angel guides Dante to Purgatory, the place where less-than-mortal sins could be atoned for. It is also, according to the theology of the time, where non-Christians and un-baptized souls spend eternity because they were not permitted to enter Heaven.

Finally, Dante is guided to Heaven where he is taken before the throne of God.

Boccaccio (1313-1375) wrote one hundred tales together known as **The Decameron**. The unifying idea of the collection was that a group of Italians, fleeing to a farmhouse outside Florence to avoid an outbreak of plague, told the stories to pass the time. Openly bawdy at times and beautiful at others, the stories deal with themes and characters from all social strata of the time.

It is debatable whether the Englishman **Geoffrey Chaucer** belongs in the grouping of the Middle Ages, because he appears late in the period and his work describes characteristics of the Renaissance: the middle class was on the rise, travel was common, and the church was corrupt. All these themes are part of his famous collection, **The Canterbury Tales**. No matter in which period Chaucer is placed, his works are important to English literature. They were the first stories of lasting value to be written in a language recognizable as English.

It is, to be precise, **Middle English** in which Chaucer wrote. Difficult to read today, though not impossible, it was, unfortunately, difficult to read only a matter of years after Chaucer's death. English was a rapidly evolving language then. In any event, his stories detail English life of the 1300s, from society and politics to economics and religion.

The Canterbury Tales begins with a prologue that sets the scene:

> Whan that Aprille with his shoures soote
> The droghte of March hath perced to roote,
> And bathed every veyne in swich licour
> Of which vertu engendred is the flour;
> Whan Zephirus eek with his sweete breeth
> Inspired hath in every holt and heeth
> The tendre croppes, and the yonge sonne
> hath in the Ram his half cours yronne,
> And smale foweles maken melodye,
> That slepen al the nyght with open eye,
> So priketh hem nature in hir corages,
> Than longen folk to goon on pilgrimages,
> And palmeres for to seken strange strondes,
> To ferne halwes kowthe in sondry londes;
> And specially from every shires ende
> Of Engelond to Caunterbury they sende,
> The hooly, blisful martir for to seke
> That hem hat holpen when that they were seeke.

Every spring, religious pilgrims traveled from London down to Canterbury and the Shrine of St. Thomas á Becket. One April day, Chaucer arrived at an inn on the city limits to await the start of such a pilgrimage, so the story goes. Twenty-nine other pilgrims also arrived at the inn that day, and they agreed to admit Chaucer to their group. Before retiring for the night, all agreed to a contest. Each person on the trip would tell two tales going down to Canterbury and two coming back. Then, upon returning to the starting point at the inn, they would vote for the best story and best story-teller. The winners were to receive a sumptuous meal, courtesy of the innkeeper. The book was never finished (probably fortunate for Chaucer because it would have meant creating 116 different tales), but every character on the pilgrimage told one tale. There are 29 tales altogether. Among the most important tales are:

- ***The Nun's Priest's Tale*** (allegory)

- ***The Franklin's Tale***

- ***The Pardoner's Tale***

- ***The Merchant's Tale***

- ***The Wife of Bath's Tale***, about a knight who rapes a beautiful maiden. King Arthur hears about it and summons him. Since the crime dealt with a woman, the queen asks Arthur to let her sentence him. The knight's sentence is to find the answer to the question, "What do women desire most?" or to die. The queen gives him a year to find out. The knight hears many things as he travels the land in search of the answer—money, jewels, clothes—but he never finds an answer all can agree upon. He returns dejectedly to the royal court a year later, but on his way comes upon the ugliest old woman he has ever seen. She says that she will tell him the answer to his question provided he will do anything she asks. With nothing to lose, he agrees. When called upon by the queen, the knight gives her the answer the old woman supplied, that women most desire to dominate their husbands. The queen and ladies cannot disagree with him, and the knight is spared. The hag speaks up about her help to him and his promise. The knight, afraid to incur the queen's wrath with a new deed of dishonor, is forced to submit to the hag's wish that he be her loving husband forever. With him in bed that night, the hag attempts to seduce him, but he is disgusted by her awful looks and age. The old woman asks him, "Would you rather have a beautiful, lecherous wife or an ugly, faithful one." She then begs him to turn toward her and kiss her. When he turns over, he finds her transformed into a beautiful woman.

• •

At this point, stop to try some sample CLEP examination questions that will test your comprehension of major works and authors from the beginnings of literature with Homer through the Middle Ages.

1.   The "face that launched a thousand ships" was that of

   (A)   Aphrodite
   (B)   Helen
   (C)   Paris
   (D)   Agamemnon
   (E)   Hera

ANSWER: A thousand Greek ships sailed from Aulis to attack Troy, whose prince, Paris, had stolen the most beautiful woman on earth, Helen, from her husband, Menelaus. The answer is (B). Aphrodite and Hera were goddesses involved in the Olympian tiff over the Golden Apple inscribed "To The Fairest," but it was not their faces the Greeks and Trojans went to war over. Paris captured Helen and took her away. Agamemnon led the Greek ships to Troy.

2.   Which of the following works is NOT an epic?

   (A)   Boccaccio's **Decameron**
   (B)   Vergil's **Aeneid**
   (C)   Homer's **Odyssey**
   (D)   Dante's **Divine Comedy**
   (E)   Milton's **Paradise Lost**

ANSWER: A series of tales about people from all walks of life, **The Decameron** cannot be an epic. (A) is the correct answer. Epics require characters of high station as one criterion, and all the other works listed here meet this requirement.

3.   Whan that Aprille with his shoures soote
   The droghte of march hath perced to the roote,
   And bathed every veyne in swich licour
   Of which vertu engendred is the flour;

   The passage above is written in

   (A)   Old English
   (B)   terza rima
   (C)   Gaelic
   (D)   Middle English
   (E)   Scottish

ANSWER: This passage is the opening to **The Canterbury Tales** by Chaucer, whose language was Middle English. The correct answer is (D). Old English is not recognizable as English and is impossible for those without special training to understand. Terza rima is a special kind of rhyme scheme, and this passage is not an example of it. We have not studied any literature in either Gaelic or Scottish; therefore, (A), (B), (C) and (E) would all be illogical and incorrect choices.

26

RENAISSANCE

William Shakespeare (1564-1616) is acknowledged the greatest writer of English. His plays exhibit boundless knowledge of topics from law, seamanship, play production, and history to chivalry, philosophy, religion, and medicine. Shakespeare's greatest insight was into the human mind. While he could physically set the stage for dramas of many different kinds of people and many places, his characters' thorough psychological development and their interactions are so logical and lifelike that one thinks they have been merely copied from life. As actor, writer and director, Shakespeare understood the workings of drama and applied them to his creative craft. More critical writing has been set down about Shakespeare than any other writer in any language. In fact, his plays are so transcendent in their portrayal of human nature, situations, and emotions that they have been translated into most languages and are regularly performed around the world.

Shakespeare borrowed many of the plots for his plays from other sources: mythology, folk tales, the Italian *commedia dell'arte* (a kind of early Renaissance bawdy show), even Boccaccio's *Decameron*. But, as the critic John Gassner put it, "It is by the shaping of the material and the bodying forth in language that a crude tale can be made into a profound work of art." Through his acute vision of life, the human mind, and the various pursuits of men, Shakespeare took the crude tales of his predecessors, Chaucer among them, and created thirty-eight plays of lasting value. That is why Shakespeare is among the writers with which CLEP students must be familiar if they are going to achieve on the humanities examination.

Shakespeare's plays are classified by four main types. You should be familiar with the types by name and definition.

The **comedies** are plays which have denouements favorable to the protagonists, or loosely, "the good guys." Although the events of the plays may include death, suffering, sorrow, illness, bad luck, or any kind of unfavorable occurrence, the ending leaves the protagonists in happy circumstances. Note well that comedy in this sense does not mean funny; it means a more or less happy ending. Among the comedies that Shakespeare wrote are the following:

- *A Midsummer Night's Dream*, the story of mismatched lovers and mischievous fairies in the forests
- *The Merchant of Venice*, in which a merchant who borrows money and pledges his flesh as collateral is saved from death at the hands of the lender when the cargo ships sink
- *The Comedy of Errors*, the reunion of two sets of long-lost twin brothers
- *The Taming of the Shrew*
- *The Two Gentlemen of Verona*
- *As You Like It*
- *Much Ado About Nothing*
- *Twelfth Night*
- *The Merry Wives of Windsor*
- *All's Well That Ends Well*
- *Measure for Measure*
- *Love's Labour's Lost*

Tragedy is the converse of comedy in its classical definition. A play may be called a tragedy when the protagonist reaches an unfavorable end, usually death. The denouement is unfortunate for the hero or heroes. Shakespeare's tragedies are among the most poignant written, and they include the following:

- **Hamlet**, a play about the murder of a king and his son's responsibility to avenge it

- **Romeo and Juliet**, in which "star-crossed" lovers come from feuding families, and circumstances bring about their double suicide

- **Othello**, the murder of a faithful, loving queen by her enraged, jealous husband over rumors that later prove false

- **Macbeth**

- **King Lear**

- **Titus Andronicus**

- **Julius Caesar**

- **Anthony and Cleopatra**

- **Coriolanus**

- **Timon of Athens**

- **Troilus and Cressida**

The **history plays** that Shakespeare wrote take events of English royal history for their subjects. While the actual words of the characters are fictionalized, the events are largely true. Some characters are Shakespeare's own, such as the clownish Falstaff, a knight of the **Henry IV** plays. Among the history plays of Shakespeare are the following:

- **Henry VI, Parts I, II and III**

- **Richard II**, the story of the "Sun King," who was more concerned with the trappings of royalty than ruling well and was overthrown by Henry Bolingbroke (King Henry IV)

- **Henry IV, Part I**, the solidification of Bolingbroke's hold on the throne and **Henry IV, Part II**, the succession of Bolingbroke's son as the second Tudor king

- **Richard III**

- **King John**

- **Henry V**

- **Henry VIII**

Shakespeare's **romances** are a special group. They can not be classified as comedy or tragedy, although they contain elements of both. Their endings are cloudy; the protagonists are not in completely tragic circumstances, but they are not fully happy, either. Lovers often come together in them, but never marry; a death may intervene in the fun, but it never puts an end to the relationships. Plays by Shakespeare that we consider romances are as follows:

- **The Winter's Tale**

- **The Tempest**

- **Cymbeline**

- **Pericles**

Above all Shakespeare's works—he wrote poetry as well as plays—**Hamlet** stands out as the most compelling, deepest, most psychologically developed, most cohesive and certainly the most eloquent piece of literature. Questions concerning Hamlet's plot and characters are sure to be found on any CLEP humanities examination. The scene opens in Elsinore, Denmark, the royal castle where a coronation festival is being held. Claudius, brother of the late King Hamlet, has married the widowed queen, Gertrude, and assumed the throne. But all is not happy in Elsinore. Soldiers standing guard on the midnight shift report that a ghost, that of King Hamlet, appears every night but refuses to communicate. Prince Hamlet, his son, is called to the battlements to try to learn the secret of the ghost's restive wanderings. Hamlet, mournful and suspicious of the activities of his uncle and mother since the death, can not understand the marriage of Claudius and Gertrude and the gaiety so soon after the king's death.

The ghost reappears but refuses to speak except to Hamlet. The ghost tells Hamlet that Claudius poisoned him, then married the queen and assumed the Danish throne. The ghost calls upon Hamlet to avenge his murder.

The young prince immediately begins planning how to kill Claudius. But before long, doubts about his own ability to do the deed creep into Hamlet's mind. Whatever the reason, Hamlet consistently finds excuses to postpone his killing of Claudius. He feigns going mad because of grief, buying time while trying to find some way to prove Claudius' guilt. Indeed, the ruse makes Claudius suspicious of the prince's knowledge of the murder, and the new king makes his own plans to dispose of young Hamlet.

At this juncture, some traveling actors arrive at Elsinore, and a play is announced. Hamlet secretly works with the actors, first coaching them in dramatic skills, then arranging for them to act out the murder of King Hamlet. "The play's the thing," Hamlet says, "wherein I'll catch the conscience of the king." Hamlet, unsure of his actions, feels silly and inadequate for not having avenged his father's death right after the appearance of the ghost. He contemplates suicide to avoid the heavy responsibility. "To be or not to be, that is the question," he says in a beautiful **soliloquy** (a character's speech while alone on stage that communicates his inner thoughts).

The "play within the play" takes place. When Claudius sees the re-enactment of King Hamlet's murder, he becomes completely unnerved. He runs screaming from the darkened hall, and the members of the court scatter in fright. Hamlet exults, feeling that the ghost's story has been confirmed, and chases after Claudius, sword in hand. He finds Claudius in the royal chapel, apparently kneeling in prayer. The prince's purpose is blunted again, this time because he fears Claudius would go straight to heaven if killed while praying for forgiveness. Instead, Hamlet runs to his mother's chambers. The situation is ironic, because when Hamlet is gone, Claudius says to himself that no matter how hard he tries to pray for forgiveness he can not. The blackness of the murder fouls him so completely he can make no spiritual contact with heaven.

Hamlet confronts his mother in her room and chastises her hotly for her unseemly actions following King Hamlet's death. In the room, Hamlet notices someone is behind the curtains eavesdropping. Hamlet assumes the eavesdropper to be Claudius and in rage stabs through the curtains. The eavesdropper turns out to be Polonius, the king's old aide and father of Hamlet's beloved, Ophelia. While Polonius deserves his fate for meddling, both Hamlet and the queen know it is also murder. Hamlet continues his pretended madness to avoid arrest.

The king, now fully aware of Hamlet's knowledge of the usurpation of the throne, plots the prince's death. A war between Poland and Norway is imminent. Claudius decides to send Hamlet, accompanied by his schoolmates and former friends, Rosencrantz and Guildenstern, to England supposedly to secure the alliance of England and Denmark. Rosencrantz and Guildenstern betray their former friend Hamlet; in the employ of the king they attempt to force out of him what the prince knows about the king's murder. However, Hamlet recognizes their motives and tells nothing. By Claudius' order, Hamlet, accompanied by the turncoat schoolmates, is to bear a letter of greeting to the king of England. In truth, however, the letter is not a greeting but one asking a favor. Kill Hamlet as a boon to the Danish King, it reads.

Hamlet, along with Rosencrantz and Guildenstern, sails for England, and during the voyage the prince learns of the plot. He replaces his name in the letter with those of Rosencrantz and Guildenstern, and the traitorous chums are killed in England. Hamlet secretly journeys back to Elsinore.

While he is away from Denmark, Ophelia commits suicide. Whether the suicide is over the death of her father, the supposed loss of her beloved Hamlet, or the brutal circumstances of having her lover murder her father, no one is quite sure. The death of the lovely girl brings her brother, Laertes, home from college in Paris. Claudius seizes the opportunity to make him an ally by stressing Hamlet to be the cause of both Polonius' and Ophelia's deaths. Naturally, when Hamlet returns in the middle of Ophelia's funeral, the conflict comes to a head. Laertes, bereaved of father and sister, meets Hamlet, bereaved of father and lover. The graveside fight is stopped by Claudius, who suggests a contest of simple fencing to settle the feud. Claudius' designs are to eliminate Hamlet once and for all. He arranges for Laertes to fence with a foil with no protective tip at the end; also, the sharp foil will be dipped in a quick-acting poison for which no antidote exists. On top of that, Claudius decides to present a cup of wine laced with poison to the victor, should it be Hamlet.

The match takes place. Hamlet easily defeats Laertes for the first two out of three points. Even though Laertes is armed with the poisoned foil, he can not touch the prince with it. After the second point, Gertrude salutes her son with a drink of wine—from the cup Claudius has poisoned. Laertes, during the break, attacks without warning or reason and wounds Hamlet with the poisoned foil. All becomes suddenly clear to the court. The prince attacks Laertes and exchanges foils in the scuffle, then stabs his one-time friend to death. Gertrude falls over dead, pointing to the poisoned cup. Hamlet, mortally wounded, is finally angered enough to kill the treacherous Claudius.

In a poignant final scene, Hamlet dies in the arms of his only remaining friend, a schoolmate and philosopher, Horatio, who had stood beside the prince throughout the drama. Fortinbras, King of Norway, marches into Elsinore fresh from vanquishing the Poles, and praises the young prince for his goodness and nobility.

• •

Now, once again try some CLEP examination questions. They should measure your understanding of some of the fundamentals concerning Shakespeare.

Questions 1 and 2 refer to the following passage:

> To be or not to be—that is the question:
> Whether 'tis nobler in the mind to suffer
> The slings and arrows of outrageous fortune
> Or to take arms against a sea of troubles
> And by opposing end them.

1. The lines above are spoken by which Shakespearean character?

   (A) Othello
   (B) Romeo
   (C) Hamlet
   (D) Macbeth
   (E) Juliet

ANSWER: (C) Hamlet, in a famous soliloquy on the courage to face life's bad times, is the speaker. This is a passage you must be able to recognize by memory. It is an easy one to remember and is often-quoted.

2. The lines are written in

   (A) blank verse
   (B) terza rima
   (C) alexandrine
   (D) heroic couplet
   (E) free verse

ANSWER: (A) Practically all of Shakespeare's plays are blank verse, which is unrhymed iambic pentameter. None of the other kinds of lines can possibly apply to the selection given. If you had trouble with this answer or cannot remember the meaning of each choice for question two, review the section on fundamentals of poetry.

3. Which of the following plays by William Shakespeare is not a comedy?

   (A) *A Midsummer Night's Dream*
   (B) *Henry IV, Part I*
   (C) *Twelfth Night*
   (D) *The Merchant of Venice*
   (E) *The Comedy of Errors*

ANSWER: (B) *Henry IV, Part I* is a history play, not a comedy. Therefore, the correct choice is (B). All the other plays are comedies. They contain a favorable ending for the protagonist or protagonists.

NEOCLASSICAL PERIOD

The Renaissance is largely counted as finished by the year 1625, when thinkers and writers of the time took on new goals. England underwent political change with the coming to power of Oliver Cromwell, a Puritan of the period who was dictator. The theatres were closed, and all other lavish kinds of art were forbidden. An austere outlook on life, refocused from humanism back to the spiritual, scientific, rational values, took hold, much as it had with the ancient Greeks. This was a new classical period and hence the name for it is **Neoclassical Period**. "Neo" is a Latin prefix meaning "new." Three writers excelled in the period: John Milton, Alexander Pope, and Jonathan Swift.

John Milton (1608-1674) is held by many scholars to be the second-greatest writer of English literature, next only to Shakespeare. He is best known for his epic poem, *Paradise Lost*, which tells of a war for control of the universe between one faction led by God and Jesus and another led by the angel Lucifer. It is wrapped up with the story of the creation and Adam and Eve. The story details the holy history of the first man and woman, the founders of the race of Christians. It is written in iambic pentameter, in a very educated, lofty tone. All these things qualify *Paradise Lost* as an epic. In the poem, God and Jesus vanquish Lucifer and his rebellious angels, consigning them to hell for eternity. The corruption and salvation of man are explained through the action.

In his own right, Milton was a genius in construction of verse. Matched with extensive knowledge and understanding of religion and politics, his ability as poet made him an all-time great in English literature. He wrote sonnets, in both Latin and English, as well as political pamphlets. Among his most notable works are *Paradise Lost*, *Paradise Regained*, and

Samson Agonistes. Milton's work popularized epic form, but his was the last great epic written in the English language.

Alexander Pope (1688-1744) was a brilliant mind trapped in a disfigured body. That internal conflict contributed much to making Pope the biting, devastating satirist he was. It probably forced him to make the most of his abilities as a philosopher. Pope, in his philosophical poems such as ***Essay on Man*** and ***Essay on Criticism***, created phrases that are among our language's most-quoted. Pope is chiefly remembered for his scathing satire on social customs, politics, even other writers, as exemplified by his mock epic poem, ***The Rape of the Lock***. **The Rape of the Lock** made fun of the epic form that was so popular yet so poorly written during his lifetime; it also ridicules the affected manners considered fashionable in the English society of his time.

Alexander Pope at an early age translated ***The Iliad*** and ***The Odyssey*** into English in heroic couplet. This form he mastered so well that he remains the acknowledged king of that verse form to this day.

Jonathan Swift (1667-1745), a contemporary of Pope, wrote in a satirical, sometimes bitter tone. An example of his outrageous and outraged wit that is often quoted for CLEP examinations, is his suggestion that Irish children be sold for food as a solution to famine in ***A Modest Proposal***, a pamphlet. His most widely read work is ***Gulliver's Travels***. In it a shipwrecked sailor is washed up on a beach in a land of tiny human beings know as Lilliput. While read as a children's book by many, ***Gulliver's Travels*** is actually a masterful satire of humans in general and Swift's countrymen in particular.

ROMANTICISM

During the course of history, for every swing public opinion takes in one direction, there is just as great a swing in the other direction. It was the same for neoclassicism. As valuable and as fine as the works of Milton, Pope, and Swift were, their style and subjects swung out of fashion. A new movement of literary thought replaced neoclassicism, **romanticism**. No longer was reason the basis for writings, nor lofty expression of classic heroic couplet the vehicle. No more were there written epics and poetry and stories of the upper classes. **Romanticism** saw its proper subject as common man in the natural world, and it spoke most often in the language of the commoner.

One of the early champions of romantic literature was **William Wordsworth** (1170-1850), an Englishman from the beautiful countryside known as the Lake District. Wordsworth wrote of the beauty and truth embodied in nature, and conversely, of the corruptive nature of city life. Like other romantics of the 18th century, Wordsworth believed man to be a naturally good creature who is corrupted by an artificial urban environment. He teamed with contemporary **Samuel Taylor Coleridge** (1772-1834) to publish a book known as ***Lyrical Ballads***, a collection of some of their poems. In a later printing of the book, Wordsworth wrote a preface, "Preface to Lyrical Ballads," explaining his theories of poetry, which included writing about common life in a "selection of language really used by men." His poems **"The Reverie of Poor Susan," "The Old Cumberland Beggar," "Lines Written in Early Spring,"** and **"Composed Upon Westmeinster Bridge"** all exemplify the romantic purpose expressed in the "Preface." Nevertheless, eloquence was no stranger to Wordsworth. Some of his poems, notably **"Tintern Abbey," "Ode: Intimations of Immorality"** and the long, autobiographical **"The Prelude,"** demonstrate Wordsworth's ability to coordinate English to inspire high emotion with common vocabulary.

Coleridge wrote relatively few poems, although he did write a great deal of Shakespearean criticism that is still studied for its insight. The poetry Coleridge did create was of high quality, for example, his single contribution to ***Lyrical Ballads***, ***The Rime of the Ancient Mariner***. Other notable poetic accomplishments of Coleridge were **"Christabel"** and the unfinished

"Kubla Khan." *The Rime of the Ancient Mariner* tells the story of a sailor who for sport shoots an albatross, bringing down the wrath of God and nature on the ship and crew. The other crew members die, and the sailor is tortured by thirst and loneliness. Only when he repents of his misdeed does the wind blow his ship back to land. Salvation is the theme of the work. It is romantic in style and thought.

George Gordon Byron, known better as **Lord Byron** (1788-1824), was a contemporary of Wordsworth and Shelley. He, too, wrote poems of nature; however, his are notable for their power of description. Byron had a great zest for life, and paradoxically it was his colorful humanity that made him superhuman. The idea of the Byronic hero stems from his writings; it is the notion of physical beauty, strong emotion and simple vitality in man. Byron's best known works are the long poem *Childe Harold's Pilgrimage* and *Don Juan*. (Do not confuse this with the Spanish poet Cervantes' *Don Juan*; Byron's character is pronounced "ew-an," as in "jewel").

"I have loved the principle of beauty in all things," wrote **John Keats** (1795-1821), another of England's 19th century romantic poets. Like Byron, Keats had a talent for descriptive verse. His did not arise from exuberance for life, though. It came from a state of mind that Keats dubbed "negative capability," or the quality of "being in uncertainties, mysteries, doubts, without any irritable reaching after fact and reason." **"Ode on a Grecian Urn"** is perhaps his best known poem, and it is certainly one of the most frequently quoted poems of the English language. Other important poetic works by Keats are **"La Belle Dame sans Merci," "Ode to a Nightingale,"** and *Endymion*.

When an early volume of Keats' poetry was critically assailed, **Percy Bysshe Shelley** (1792-1822) defended his friend's work. Shelley, one of the great poets of the Romantic Period in England, was later moved to write *Adonais*, a poetic defense of Keats, because he felt the harsh criticism had led to Keats' early death. The work demonstrates the keen sense of spiritual feeling of which Shelley was capable, and which he applied to his voluminous writings. Shelley differs from other romantics only in that he saw physical beauty as a clue to the true beauty, that of the soul. Among Shelley's best poems are **"Ode to the West Wind"** and **"To a Skylark."**

The romantic characteristics of English writers were first reflected in America by writers who were also philosophers. With **Ralph Waldo Emerson** (1803-1882) and **Henry David Thoreau** (1817-1862), the perception of nature as beneficent and the belief that man is spiritually good had their introduction into American thought. Both Emerson and Thoreau were New Englanders; they were neighbors and friends in Massachusetts.

Emerson is best know for his lectures and essays. His 1841 book, *Essays*, contains **"Self-Reliance"** and **"Experience,"** two treatises on the need for each individual to have a personal understanding of his spiritual light. Emerson believed, as did other **transcendentalists** of the time, that there is truth in a spiritual level of existence that is beyond the mere physical world. Emerson also wrote some very good, but altogether introspective, solemn poetry. Among the notable poems are **"Days"** and **"The Snow-Storm."**

Thoreau, like Emerson, had great respect for nature. Indeed, the mention of his name always brings to mind his most famous work, a journal called *Walden*. Disenchanted with society, Thoreau took to the woods near Walden Pond, Massachusetts, where he lived alone in a small house for slightly more than two years. His purpose was to demonstrate that the best life is the independent, self-reliant one. He built his own house, grew his own organic food, read the classics, studied the woods about him and serenely contemplated life during his self-imposed solitude. Thoreau did not ignore his neighbors, nor was he anti-social. He believed in freedom and democracy, but on a very individual level. Once, he refused to pay a tax he said helped support the war against Mexico and cited his conscience as his guide. Even though he paid other taxes that were not supportive of evil, Thoreau served a stint in jail for his action. The incident gave rise to another well-known work, ***On the Duty of Civil Disobedience***. It is an eloquent essay defending the right and moral duty of any citizen, to have no part of a law or custom inherent of evil. Thoreau advocated in the essay a personal policy of passive resistance to policies which truly offend one's conscience. Such thought matches the teachings of Mohandas Gandhi, who led India to freedom with the idea, and Leo Tolstoy, a Russian social reformer, writer, and philosopher of the late 19th century.

The romantic movement in England had even stronger reflections in America. American writers were finally coming into world recognition by the mid-1800's, led by **Walt Whitman** (1819-1892). Whitman is classified a romantic because he believed in man as an essentially good creature, and because he wrote in the language of common people. Whitman's spelling and grammar, in fact, are frequently incorrect, as far as the rules of language are concerned. But to correct his lines is to destroy them because they vibrate with the intense emotions of an uninhibited, perceptive man. Whitman's "lack of inhibition" was not confined to grammar, either. He wrote freely about love between people of all sexes and races. Though the love he expressed was spiritual, his verse was unashamedly sensuous and shocking for the strict times. Whitman's huge volume of poetry, ***Leaves of Grass***, contains chapters of poems named after native American grasses and covers a multitude of subjects from love to war to nature. Whitman, seeing everything as part of a functioning cosmic system, revered nature as a mother and brother to men. Some important single poems by Whitman are ***Song of Myself***, ***Crossing Brooklyn Ferry***, and ***There Was a Child Went Forth***.

Emily Dickinson (1830-1886) was a contemporary of Whitman, although the two never met (if, indeed, they ever read one another's works; Dickinson lived in the household of her Puritan minister father, where such things as Whitman's poems probably would have been forbidden). Only a few of Dickinson's poems were ever published during her lifetime. Scholars speculate frequently about her personal life because of the intensity of feeling in her poems. It is known that Dickinson knew a minister from Philadelphia, and that they cared for each other more than casually. A few scholars conjecture that, denied the already married preacher, Dickinson withdrew from all social life. At 23, she began leading a life of solitude and almost never left the house during her last 10 to 15 years. Punctuation, primarily in the form of commas and dashes, is not for grammar's sake in Dickinson's poetry. Instead, it emphasizes particular words and phrases, separates them from others in the lines, even stresses the separate meanings of two words or phrases while at the same time linking them. Such craftsmanship in poetry is seldom seen; and the effect is colorful, vivid images, strong emotion, and hence, strong communication between author and reader. Death, religion, and the nature of immortality figure prominently as subjects of Dickinson's verse, and capture scenes of nature as carefully as the most sophisticated photographer does—but without the wordiness of an Audubon or the anarchy of a Whitman. **"Because I could not stop for death," "There is a certain slant of light," "I heard a buzz when I died," "I taste a liquor never brewed"** and **"The heart asks pleasure first"** demonstrate the best qualities of America's greatest female poet. None of her poems is titled; all are designated by first lines.

Edgar Allen Poe (1809-1849) may be loosely classified with the romantics. His works, chiefly short stories and poems, rely heavily upon imagination and imagery. Poe pioneered the development of the short story, an exclusively American contribution to literature, and he is still among the great writers of the genre. Poe led a hard life. He was an adopted orphan, disinherited by his foster father. His wife died at an early age. He had an alcohol problem. He found it difficult to keep working, whether at school or at a job. Poe's vision was a morbid one, and his best and best-known works deal with such subjects as death, torture, and the supernatural. Mental illness and criminal behavior frequently turn up in his writings. Nevertheless, his works are enlightening, thrilling, and entertaining; what more can the reader ask from an author? His short stories include **"The Telltale Heart," "The Cask of Amontillado,"** and the collection, ***The Murders of the Rue Morgue***. His poems, frightening and inspiring, include **"The Raven," "For Annie," "The Bells,"** and **"Annabel Lee."**

Another American who wrote during the 1800s and remains among America's greats is **Mark Twain** (1835-1910). His real name was Samuel Langhorne Clemens. A Midwesterner from Hannibal, Missouri, he lived through the settling of the West, the Civil War, and the blossoming of the United States. Therefore, he held a special vision of America and its people. Twain worked at a variety of jobs before becoming a writer, including river pilot on the Mississippi. It was from that profession's terminology for measuring the depth of the channel that he took his pen name. After attempting prospecting in Nevada with his brother, he began writing for a newspaper and started down the road to fame as a journalist. His work took him all over the world, and his keen perception of people provided him grist for his story mill. Twain wrote short stories and novels, all of which contain an element of humor that remains as funny today as it was when written. Twain had a flair for the dramatic as well, and described scenes so powerfully that he brings his readers to tears at times in *Tom Sawyer* and *Huckleberry Finn*. Both books are American classics, and do not deserve the label, "children's books," that some people assign them. *Huckleberry Finn* in particular, with its insights into slavery and social customs, is as potent or more so for the adult as for the child with its picture of America and Americans in the ante-bellum period. *A Connecticut Yankee in King Arthur's Court* takes its hero back in time to medieval days, and makes fun of Arthurian legends while satirizing the 1800s. *Life on the Mississippi* is Twain's autobiographical account of his youth, during which he lived along the Mississippi River. Twain's short stories are usually humorous vignettes of 19th century America. "The Celebrated Jumping Frog of Calaveras County" is perhaps the best known. Twain mastered the art of reproducing dialect on paper, for example, the American Negro slave speech of Jim from *Huckleberry Finn*.

America had its romantic novelists, as well as poets and journalists. Among them were **Nathaniel Hawthorne** (1804-1864) and **Herman Melville** (1819-1891). The fact that both were New Englanders figures strongly in the subject and style of their works.

Hawthorne achieved fame for his book *The Scarlet Letter*, the story of a young woman, Hester Prynne, who became pregnant out of wedlock by a Puritan minister, Reverend Dimmesdale. To her death, Hester protected the identity of the man who "sinned" with her, even though she was forced by law to wear the bright red letter "A" on her clothing for her entire life to signify her adultery. *The House of the Seven Gables* is another well-known Hawthorne novel. In all of his works, Hawthorne's literary study of allegory shines through. Spenser and Bunyan, two famous writers of allegory, were his favorites. The Hawthorne short story "Young Goodman Brown" is an allegory of blossoming corruption in a young New England man. While *The Scarlet Letter* has characters whose names give some insight into their natures, it is not true allegory; the characters have complete development as people, not as representations of ideas. This can be seen as a link between the allegory, the ancient method of connecting a story with a moral, and symbolism, a new but then imperfect method of communicating verbally inexpressible truth.

Melville traveled the world, usually as a sailor, and from his shipboard experiences he drew the material for his greatest works, the novels *Moby Dick* and *Billy Budd*. While it was not a particularly popular novel, *Moby Dick* is clearly Melville's best effort. It is the story of a young sailor who opens the book, saying "Call me Ishmael." Even though we may call the storyteller Ishmael, there is little doubt that it is Melville recounting some of his experiences from life aboard whaling boats in the South Pacific. *Moby Dick* tells the tale of Captain Ahab and his whaling ship, the Pequod. Ahab pursued the business of whaling with but one goal in mind: to kill the great white whale that indirectly caused the loss of his leg some years before. Ishmael and the crew sailed with Ahab on his final journey, during which the whale sank the Pequod and dragged Ahab, in a tangled harpoon line, to a watery death. Many critics see Moby Dick as symbolic of the human struggle against evil and fate. Both Melville and Hawthorne, with their New England backgrounds, were influenced by the doctrine of predestination in their religion. The Puritans believed that only the "elect" could enter heaven, regardless of their behavior on earth. Even if a man was a perfectly good soul, he could not enter the kingdom unless he was one of the elect, the Puritan thinking went. **The Scarlet Letter** and **Moby Dick** both tackle this theme. Melville's **Billy Budd**, the story of a good, young sailor wrongly convicted and hanged aboard his ship is a poignant story also along these lines. Billy, sad but with a smile on his face, volunteers to climb the rigging to the yardarm, where he is to be hanged.

REALISM AND NATURALISM

The give and take between science and art gave again toward science in the late 19th and early 20th centuries, when a man named **Charles Darwin** permanently upset the artistic apple cart. Humans, he carefully reasoned, were not the direct creation of heaven, but rather the end product of billions of years of evolution, natural selection, and survival of the fittest. The concurrent rise of the middle class merchant society we still have forced the world to look at man's problems through middle class eyes. Two movements arose from these social developments: realism and naturalism.

The middle to late 1800s saw the rise of the new literary schools in Europe (they came later to America). The Englishman **Charles Dickens** (1812-1870) was one of the foremost writers of realism. The object of **realism** is to recreate life in art without exaggeration or euphemism. Dickens' realism shows up best in his representations of the life of the poor people in England during his times. **David Copperfield** and **Oliver Twist** are stories about abused, poor, parentless children. **A Christmas Carol** contrasts rich Ebenezer Scrooge with poor Bob Cratchit and family. **Great Expectations** traces the life of a poor country boy, Pip, through his transformation and maturation as the recipient of an anonymously bequeathed fortune. **A Tale of Two Cities**, a story of the French Revolution, and **Pickwick Papers**, a newspaper serial, were other important works of Dickens.

Realism made its way into drama through a Norwegian playwright named **Henrik Ibsen** (1828-1906). During Ibsen's lifetime, society underwent major changes. The middle class asserted itself as the dominant social force of the world. The ideas of socialism and equal rights for women were born and spread. Darwin published his theory of evolution, destroying the long-held notion that man was the special creation of God. It is no surprise, then, that such topics found their way into the theatre. Prose became the language of comedy and tragedy, replacing the poetic lines of earlier drama. Social situations became proper subjects of plays—social situations involving the middle and lower classes instead of the royalty, clergy, or aristocracy. The language written was the vernacular—the local dialect—instead of pompous, high-born declamation; the subjects included politics and the idea that society functions, as does Darwin's nature, in the survival of the fittest. Ibsen, called "the father of modern drama," chose from all these styles and subjects for his plays, and occasionally incited riots with them. His play **Ghosts** deals with characters inflicted with venereal disease. **A Doll's House**, a perennially popular and recently topical play, takes for its subject a woman who, unable by law to borrow money, forges her ill husband's signature on a loan note to keep them solvent while he is unable to work. Later, when the husband is outraged by her all-too-necessary "crime," she walks out on him and their two children.

Realism had its best expression in the Untied States through such authors as **Henry James** (1843-1916) and **Stephen Crane** (1871-1900). Their realistic, accurate, detailed depiction of American life, is among the best.

36

James experimented with forms of realism, often telling his stories through the vision of one or more characters. This psychological viewpoint paved the way for later writers to increase the complexity and insight of their works through such devices as **stream of consciousness**, in which a character's thoughts appear on the page as they do through his or her mind. James wrote short novels, or **novellas**; and among his finest are ***Daisy Miller*** and ***The American***. James also wrote novels and short stories. His extensive travels through the United States and Europe gave him unusual insight into the American mind; he could see Americans as both a fellow and a foreigner.

Stephen Crane is associated with that branch of realism called naturalism. **Naturalism** is extreme realism that advocates scientific observation of life without idealization, and without skipping events and descriptions that may be termed "ugly." Naturalism pays great tribute to the notion of social Darwinism, or survival of the fittest in society. Crane's most highly regarded work is the short book ***The Red Badge of Courage***, which tells in naturalistic fashion how a soldier leaves home to fight in the Civil War, runs away from what he thinks is certain death in his first battle, and later, when his conscience forces him, forsakes his intent to desert, joins another outfit and becomes a hero in battle. Among several short stories by Crane, **"The Open Boat"** is widely read and held to be his best.

SYMBOLISM

Naming an author and his works as great is something we do best in hindsight. A writer's contemporaries may find him loathsome, as several of Shakespeare's did. Conversely, we may hold a current writer in esteem while future generations may ignore him. That is why we have trouble classifying modern writers "great" or "insignificant" when we study them; the future will judge the lasting value of their works.

We can, nevertheless, perceive a movement among the early 20th century authors, particularly the poets, and pick out the best writers. The movement is symbolism, which you will recall from our lesson in literary terms is the communication of ideas and truths that are impossible to verbalize. The communication is through symbols, which connote certain feelings and instinctive knowledge in the readers' mind. The early part of our century saw great interest in psychology, the study of the mind, and the healing of disordered minds (psychiatry). **Sigmund Freud** and **Carl Jung** advanced their theories of the operation of the human psyche, and inevitably their studies affected the writing and reading of literature. Freud espoused the idea of a mind divided into three parts: conscience, or super ego; conscious, or ego; and chaos, or id. He felt that once the repression and guilt of the super ego and the irrational motivation of the id could be brought to the patient's conscious scrutiny, mental problems could be cured. Jung placed his efforts into a theory of archetypes, or instincts and emotions ingrained in the collective mind of humanity since prehistoric days and called forth by the senses in day-to-day living. For example, Jung might have explained the habit of people staring at the ocean by an archetypal vision of the ocean as the home of all life on earth.

It is easy to see that literature can no longer be read only for the face value of the words.

One of the most admired of the 20th century poets is **William Butler Yeats** (1865-1939). Born in Ireland and educated in England, Yeats had a feel for the natural beauty of the land and sea of his home region; but he also had known the cosmopolitan experience and refinement of the cities of Europe. Yeats relied heavily on symbolism to communicate the truths he felt. One of the more popular themes in Yeat's poetry is the search for immortality by man. The theme appears in three of his important poems, **"Sailing to Byzantium," "The Second Coming,"** and **"Lapis Lazuli."**

A later English poet, **W.H. Auden** (1907-1973), is also well-known for his application of symbolism to poetry.

T. S. Eliot (1888-1964) is sometimes referred to as the creator of modern poetry. His use of experimental forms and bold, previously forbidden topics, blazed the way for poetry to strengthen its grasp of human experience. Eliot was a pioneer of free verse, liberating poetry from strict forms. He spoke, although through symbols, of themes sexual in nature. He wrote lines with obscure references to earlier literature that made his lines inaccessible to the less-educated or less-dedicated reader, but making them increasingly transcendent in their communication of thought and emotion. Eliot is most famous for his long poem in five parts, *The Waste Land*. His other important poems are **"The Love Song of J. Alfred Prufrock"** and **"The Hollow Men."** Eliot was an American by birth, yet, he was disgruntled with American thought and society, and he moved to England. He is buried in the poets' corner of Westminster Abbey, London.

In regard to the novelists of the modern period, there are so many, both British and American, writing in such divergent styles and about varying topics and themes, that it would be impossible to categorize them. Instead, the student taking the CLEP examination must rely on his own reading to give him a background. It is very likely that in school or for pleasure you have encountered the works of a great many of them, and for the purposes of your CLEP examination preparation it would be silly to do more than remind you of some frequently appearing authors and titles.

F. Scott Fitzgerald (1896-1940) wrote *The Great Gatsby*, a story of the decadent rich of Long Island, New York. Fitzgerald is recognized for his acute vision of America and Americans during the pre-Depression times of the Roaring 20's.

Ernest Hemingway (1899-1961) wrote the popular *A Farewell to Arms* and *The Old Man and the Sea*, among several other books.

William Faulkner (1897-1962), the writer of the South, has become quite popular among scholars. His popularity is based on his content, stories set in the American South about Southern society and thought; his style, the stream of consciousness is one of his favorite devices, and the complex psychological development of his characters. *Light in August* and *As I Lay Dying* receive a good deal of attention in the study of Faulkner's works.

•••••••••••••••••••••••••••••••

The following sample CLEP questions focus on writers from the period of the post-Renaissance to modern authors.

1. Which of the following is a group of neoclassical authors?

    (A)   Shakespeare, Chaucer, Twain
    (B)   Homer, Vergil, Milton
    (C)   Crane, James, Dickinson
    (D)   Defoe, Swift, Sterne
    (E)   Pope, Milton, Swift

ANSWER: The best choice for this question is (E). Pope, Milton and Swift all wrote during the so-called Age of Reason, or Neoclassical Period. The authors in (B) have in common the fact that they wrote epics, but they did so about a thousand years apart in the order given above. (C) is incorrect; these three Americans wrote during the 19th century. In (D), Swift is the only neoclassical author of the three; Defoe and Sterne wrote their early novels during the 18th century.

2.   Realism and naturalism were the artistic results of

   (A)   the Puritans
   (B)   the theory of evolution
   (C)   the American Revolution
   (D)   the Industrial Revolution
   (E)   disillusioned romantics

ANSWER: (B) is the best choice; Darwin's theory inspired a new interest in the biological aspect of life that writers reflected during the 19th and early 20th centuries. In these movements, writers sought to show real life and common people, and represented life's conflicts as survival of the fittest.

3.   Two romantic novelists from America were

   (A)   Wordsworth and Mallory
   (B)   Twain and Dickinson
   (C)   Thoreau and Emerson
   (D)   Thoreau and Melville
   (E)   Melville and Hawthorne

ANSWER: (E) is the best choice, because both Melville and Hawthorne are recognized as American romantics. At least one member of the remaining pairs of writers here is not a romantic or is not American.

There, in a nutshell, is an outline of literature. From Homer though Faulkner, the thread that ties all lasting authors together is the ability to communicate important ideas and feelings though the written word. The styles vary, prose to poetry and classicism to naturalism and symbolism; however, well-expressed content can be found in each.

If you have not read widely before now, pay special attention to the modern authors before you take the humanities examination. If you have the opportunity, read one of the books or works listed in this outline for each of the authors you are unfamiliar with. Because of the background knowledge you already possess about each, their works will be at least as interesting and certainly more worthwhile than the best popular literature available today. Using this outline as a guide, read all or part of a work by an author you have not studied before while riding the bus or eating lunch. Books containing all these works can be checked out of almost any library, large or small.

Also, if you decide you want to know more about an author or work you do not have the time to read, ask a reference librarian to suggest a good plot summary encyclopedia, such as **Master Plots**. Any reading you do on the fine literature of the world will help you to score higher on the CLEP humanities examination and will also leave you a more interesting individual.

Music Review

The most frequently asked question concerning music in the CLEP Humanities examination asks you to identify signs from musical notation. Others ask you to match famous musical compositions with their composers. Some may have you identify authors from literature with composers who were their contemporaries, countrymen or stylistic counterparts (for example, one might be asked to select romantic style authors and composers).

Therefore, this music review is written in two parts. The first covers the basics of musical notation; the second briefly surveys the history of music. Careful study of this section will allow you to add many valuable points to your exam score in humanities.

MUSICAL NOTATION

In order to pass musical compositions along from person to person and from one generation to the next, there must be a standardized form of writing them down. **Musical notation** is that form, and it is used in all Western cultures as well as some Far Eastern cultures to permanently record the directions of a composer to vocal and instrumental performers.

Let us review musical notation by building a line of music from scratch.

Written music always begins with five parallel lines drawn across the page in a group. This is called a **staff**.

A Staff

Notice that a staff is always closed at right and left by a vertical bar. There can be more than one staff to a line of music when the music is complicated, as in a symphony or a choral composition. When vocal music is written, there is a staff for the voice melody and a staff or two for the piano or accompanying instruments. When more than one staff is needed for a line of music, the staves are joined as below. This shows they are the same line of music and keeps all the performers in time with each other.

Soprano {

Alto {

When choral music, or music for choirs, is written there is one staff for the women's parts, one for the men's parts and one for the accompaniment. There can be one only for **sopranos** (high female voices), one only for **altos** (low female voices), one only for **tenors** (high male voices), one only for **basses** (low male voices) and then one or more for instrumental accompaniment. When you think how complicated an orchestra's music must be, it is easy to understand how only one line of music can take a whole page to write!

Once the staff has been drawn, it must have a clef sign placed on it to tell the performer the approximate range of the pitches for the notes. There are two clef signs: one looks like an inverted S and is called the **treble clef**. It indicates that the notes on the staff will be above the note referred to as middle C. Note that the clef sign appears on the far left of the staff.

Treble Clef

The other clef is the **bass clef**. It resembles an apostrophe followed by two bold dots, and signifies that the notes on the staff will be those below middle C. Again, note that the clef always appears all the way to the left of the staff.

Bass Clef

A clef is always the very first sign to appear on a line of music.

The next thing you will see on any line of music is the **key signature**. The key signature is a group from zero to seven **sharps** or from zero to seven **flats**.

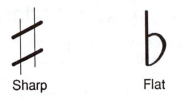

Sharp   Flat

The number and arrangement of these sharps or flats tells the musician which note on the staff shall be what we commonly refer to as "do."

Here are some examples of key signatures written on a staff:

A Major   G Minor

Two numbers written as a fraction are the next thing found written on a line of music. This is the **time signature**. The bottom number indicates what kind of note will be given one beat when the music is sung or played. The top number indicates how many beats will be written in each measure of music. A **measure** is a phrase of music, indicated by two vertical bars (one at the beginning and one at the end). Measures aid in the counting of the beat. In a given musical composition, all measures must have an equal number of full beats, except the first and last measures. Look at this example:

The 4 on the top means that there will be four beats to each measure. The 4 on the bottom of the time signature means that a ¼ note, or quarter note, gets one beat.

The next thing you will find on the staff will be **notes**. They work two ways: 1) they tell the musician the pitch he must play or sing by their placement on the staff; and, 2) they tell him, by their differing designs, how long to play or sing each pitch. Let us look at the common kinds of notes.

whole   half   quarter   eighth   sixteenth

Put staff, clef, key signature, time signature, notes, and measure together, and you have a typical line of written music.

Look at the opening line, above, from a nursery rhyme set to music. Name all the parts of the line, figure out how many beats there are to each measure, and, if you can, figure out which nursery rhyme it is.

A CONCISE HISTORY OF MUSIC

Music has been with us from the caveman who blew into seashells to the artist who plays the Stradivarius violin. Music however, never really developed into a form of expression in any complexity until it began to be written. The Greeks, who thought that mathematics and music were the keys to the secrets of existence and who believed that the planets revolved and produced a kind of heavenly harmony, were the first to write music. Theirs was primitive notation, using letters.

The next group to improve the system of writing music was the priests of the Middle Ages under Pope Gregory. Theirs combined rhythm and pitch on a fixed scale, and was a direct forerunner of our modern method of writing music. The priests under Pope Gregory wrote religious music, chants of liturgy known as **Gregorian chant**. This and all music from the Middle Ages was monophonic, that is, it was single line melody only.

Eventually, people wanted to create music of greater beauty than simple monophony. They combined melodies whose pitches did not clash and thus gave birth to counterpoint. **Counterpoint** is the playing or singing of two dissimilar but harmonizing melodies at the same time.

By the year 1,000 A.D., a monk named **Guido d'Arezzo** created the staff and named the notes in the form we know them today.

The Renaissance swept literature with great reawakening of interest in knowledge and art. This was also the case with music, and the period was marked by the rise of complex, polyphonic music. This music of intricate harmony was used primarily in church services or had religious themes. At the same time, instruments were being improved or invented, permitting ever greater, grander and more beautiful compositions and performances.

Antonio Vivaldi (1675-1741) of Italy was perhaps the greatest composer of the Renaissance period.

English composers reached their greatest height in the late Renaissance, when **Orlando Gibbons** (1583-1625) and **Henry Purcell** (1659-1695) wrote music for poetry and church services. The late Renaissance period of 1590-1700 was dominated by the Italians and English.

The 1700s, however, saw the rise of the greatest classical composers from the European continent. **Bach** (1685-1750) of Germany, a church organist, wrote complicated organ music that is unmatched today for its complexity and intensity. Surprisingly, Bach seldom had his works published or played in public.

Classicism, represented by Bach and others, is the refined, polished expression of emotion through music. The movement reached its height with **Haydn** (1732-1809) and **Mozart** (1756-1791) in the late 1700s. **Handel's *Messiah*** tells Christ's life from prophecy to resurrection, in choral and chamber music. To meet the ravenous public appetite for more and more new music, these composers wrote, all together, hundreds of symphonies, quartets, chorales, operas, and concertos.

Classicism was replaced as the dominant musical movement in the 1800s by **romanticism**, the idea that music should exclaim emotion full-strength. For example, there are the works of **Ludwig von Beethoven** (1770-1827), whose nine symphonies still tingle the spines of audiences today. His sixth symphony, known as **"Pastoral,"** and his ninth symphony, **"Choral,"** are two of the most important.

Nationalism, the expression of a country's people in music, dominated the late 1800s. Strong examples are the Teutonic operas of Germany's **Richard Wagner** (1813-1883), the compositions of Russia's **Peter Tchaikovsky** (1840-1893), and the symphonies of Bohemia's **Anton Dvorak** (1841-1904).

Opera was the national expression of Italy. It reached its highest level under **Guiseppe Verdi** (1813-1901), **Giacomo Puccini** (1858-1924), **Gioacchino Rossini** (1792-1868) and **Vincenzo Bellini** (1801-1835).

The 20th century saw the trend of nationalism continue in **Prokofiev** (1891-1953) of Russia, **Copland** (1900-1992) of the United States and **Strauss** (1864-1949) and **Hindemith** (1895-1963) of Germany. During the century, composers also wrote what might be called "international style," a style unidentifiable as to country. **Igor Stravinsky**, **Claude Debussy**, and **Maurice Ravel** can be included in that movement.

The 20th century has also seen the development of jazz, which has its roots in the ethnic music of American Negroes in the Deep South. It has gained a worldwide following, as well as the approval of musical scholars, for its ability to express emotion in wide ranges. Famous jazz composers include **Duke Ellington** and **Dizzy Gillespie**.

• •

Check your familiarity with the broad subject of music by trying some sample CLEP examination questions.

1. Study this portion of a line of music.

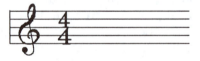

In the music that follows this notation, there will be

(A) a crescendo
(B) eighth notes
(C) four beats to each measure
(D) a repeat
(E) two sharps

ANSWER: From the information given, the best answer is (C). The time signature, the two numbers written as a fraction at the beginning of a line of music, tells how many beats there will be in each measure. It also tells which type of note gets one beat.

2. 𝄢

This symbol is a

(A) bass clef
(B) treble clef
(C) time signature
(D) flat
(E) staff

ANSWER: (A)

3. Which group of composers was Austrian?

(A) Haydn, Mozart, Schubert
(B) Copland, Gibbons, Dvorak
(C) Tchaikovsky, Puccini, Wagner
(D) Prokofiev, Wagner, Beethoven
(E) Mozart, Dvorak, Haydn

ANSWER: While there are Austrian composers included in two of these groups, the only completely Austrian group is (A).

Art Review

In a very broad sense, **art** is making and doing things skillfully. We will constrain our review of art to those things more often known as the **fine arts**: architecture, sculpture and painting.

ARCHITECTURE

Think of the things we do in buildings: sleep, eat, shop, work, play. Today, practically anything that can be done by people can be done indoors. Architecture's development through the ages is of great importance, and it is a development that must be traced to understand the past and improve the present.

The first buildings were not really buildings at all. They were the constructions of nature: caves, holes in the ground, fallen trees. Such places offered security from the elements as well as from other animals and allowed humans to develop things that would otherwise have been destroyed by the prehistoric world. People fostered religion in their early dwellings and passed it on through crude drawings on cave walls. Religion, from then to now, has been the greatest motivating force in building.

The first serious, complicated building was done by the world's first dominant civilization, Egypt. As Egypt conquered the known world around the Mediterranean Sea, it gathered tremendous wealth in precious metals and in human resources (that is to say, slaves). Egypt's society was built upon a religious hierarchy that included the pharaoh as a god, and much of the wealth went toward building religious structures, particularly tombs.

The greatest achievement of that sort was the **pyramids**. They were made of stone blocks laid in patterns upon one another reaching to a pinnacle. According to the historian Herodotus, 100,000 slaves needed twenty years to build the largest, the pyramid of Cheops.

Although they had little practical value, the **pyramids** are a lasting testament to human ingenuity and determination.

Similar structures were built around the Fertile Crescent (what is now Egypt, Israel, Syria, Jordan and Iran), but the people used different materials. Babylonians used sun-baked bricks of clay and straw to build **ziggurats**, artificial high places with temples for local deities.

The next great advancements were made when the ancient Greek civilization conquered the western world. The Greeks invented an architectural device which permitted them to create buildings of unprecedented inner size and space. The **post and lintel** easily held up the roofs of buildings, the lintel holding the roof, the post supporting it off the ground. In ancient Greece, the post was also known as the column.

There were three types of columns used by the Greeks:

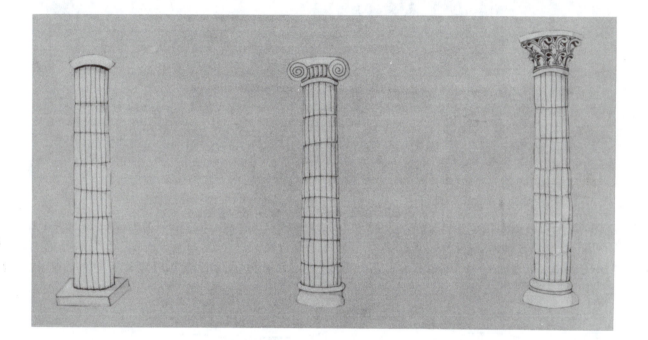

- The **Doric** column was the original, sporting a simple **capital**, or top. It was plain in its design but spectacular in its massive simplicity in those early times.

- Another type of column was the **Ionic**. Note the change in the capital. Where before there had been simply a plain circle, there were curly designs, one on each side as decoration.

- The **Corinthian** was the latest of all the Greek columns. It sported elaborate decoration at the top that resembled leaves or flourishing vegetation. Buildings with Corinthian capitals were signified as important in ancient Greek society.

As in the Egyptian times, architecture was devoted in large part to religion during the Greek period. Greek advances, then, were applied to temples for the gods, built on high places. The most famous and representative building of Greek architecture is one in Athens dating from 432 B.C., known as the Parthenon.

The Parthenon

Built of white marble, the temple was a reminder to all, which gods—the Greek—ruled the universe.

The Greeks were not confined to building temples, though. Along with market places, meeting halls and gymnasiums, they also created theatres.

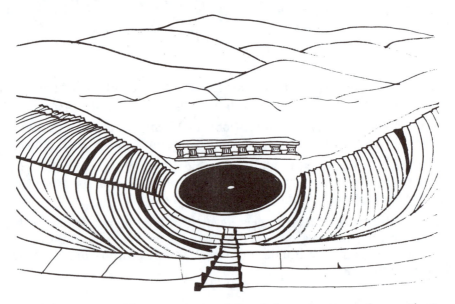

Usually constructed from marble, in a natural bowl for retention of sound, Greek theatres enabled performances of plays for large audiences

Around 180 B.C., Rome conquered Greece, and eventually the known world of the time. While militarily superior to all nations, the Romans were cultural inferiors to the Greeks and adopted almost all Greek culture—including architecture. There were two important architectural contributions by the Romans, however: the **arch** and the **vault**.

The **arch** permits large openings in buildings and supports great weight in structures not completely solid. Large, top-rounded windows are fine examples of the Roman development, as are aqueducts and old bridges.

The **vault** was brick and stone held together by cement in a dome pattern. Each piece transfers weight out from the center of the dome and down to the walls.

As in the above drawing of the Roman Pantheon, you will notice that the vault permitted wide spaces inside to be roofed over. Vaults also required massive, thick walls below to bear their weight.

In 200 A.D., the Roman Empire declined and was divided into two administrative sections. A second capital was placed in Constantinople. A new style of architecture developed there, combining the Roman and Middle Eastern elements. It was the **Byzantine** style. Look at this drawing of St. Sophia's Cathedral in Constantinople, now Istanbul, Turkey.

Note the arches in the windows and the huge dome. Also note the smooth Middle Eastern materials of mud and brick. The towers are later Moslem additions called **minarets**.

When the Roman Empire fell in 476 A.D., the world fell into the Dark Ages. Learning was not prized during the period. It is no surprise, then, that little architectural development took place. The Roman Catholic church kept learning alive.

Cities grew at the end of the Dark Ages. The Roman Catholic church was the focal point of new achievements in architecture. The Crusades again connected Europe to the rest of the world. Church builders demonstrated a penchant for great size, devising the **ribbed vault**. It permits great roofs and ceilings with fewer heavy walls and pillars. Medieval builders also developed the **flying buttress**, to shore up burdened walls.

While buttresses served to hold up the exceptionally tall walls and expansive roofs, they were also magnificent decoration.

Look at this representation of a typical Gothic cathedral. Note the flying buttresses, the pointed arches that support ribbed vault roofs.

During the Renaissance, around 2500, builders tried to combine the beauty of Roman architecture with functional need in public buildings. We call the trend **neoclassical**.

St. Paul's Cathedral in London, above, uses Roman columns, domes, and arches in its religious purpose. The effort is to inspire.

Drawing of St. Martin-in-the Fields

The church above is another example. See how the steeple has been placed on top of a building that might otherwise be a Roman temple.

A major diversion since neoclassical architecture has been **Bauhaus**. This is the modernistic school of abstract building design using lots of glass and bright metal. We might call it "modern architecture."

We have made a quick but important survey of architecture. Now let us do the same for painting and sculpture, which share many of the same characteristics.

PAINTING AND SCULPTURE

Painting began on the walls of caves. They were in the form of stick drawings, but evolved dramatically when Egypt became the dominant western civilization. Religion was the motivation and subject of works that both decorated and told stories. To the left is a photograph of the tomb of King Tutankhamon, "King Tut." The painting is on a wall. Wall paintings are known as **frescoes**. Note that while the figures are detailed and easily recognized as men, they have no perspective and show no movement.

Statues of the Egyptian period also exhibit the characteristics of no perspective and no movement.

Even in statues of animals, there is no sign of movement. For example, look at the statue referred to as *An Egyptian Cat*.

Courtesy Metropolitan Museum of Art
Purchase, 1958, Fund from Various Donors.

The highly inventive ancient Greeks overcame Egyptian shortcomings. They sought to capture nature in their statues, hence the term **naturalism**.

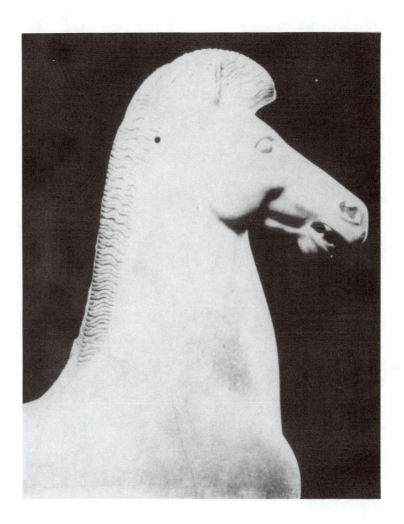

Here we have a horse from the ruins of the Acropolis. Notice the attempt to carve a naturally flowing mane, to make a smooth, proper mouth, and muscles in proportion to each other, as in life.

Greek statues were also the first to capture motion, as in the example below.

Here the goddess Athena is in mid-step, giving the viewer a sense of motion and heightened reality. It is a concept that eluded the ancient Egyptians.

Most Greek painting was applied to pottery, and exhibited the same improvements.

The Romans copied Greek art almost directly, but they did embellish it a little.

A Greek statue of **Aphrodite** was copied by later civilizations, including the Romans. The Romans called their copy, the Roman **Venus**.

There was very little Roman contribution to painting. In the eastern division of the empire there was even a slight reversion. Formal depiction of scenes, in mosaics and icons, went back from the great realistic steps of Greece to stiff figures and folds of cloth and awkward positions. Look at these examples.

In the icon above, entitled **The Virgin of Love**, look at the unreal shape of the characters' heads. There is no perspective, depth or movement.

We see the same qualities in a mosaic of the time called *The Doubt of St. Thomas*.

Just as significant as the Byzantine reversion was the huge advancement of art in Renaissance Europe. It focused on individualism and naturalism in paintings. The styles began in Italy and later spread across the continent. At first, a favorite subject was religion. Some notable portraits were of the Virgin Mary holding the baby Jesus. Boticelli's **The Virgin and Child with St. John** demonstrates the return to natural, even ideal, looking subjects in natural colors and settings.

In Leonardo Da Vinci's **Madonna and Child with St. Anne**, those characteristics are further refined.

Neither Botticelli nor Da Vinci limited himself to religious themes. Botticelli revisited Roman and Greek concentration on the human form, and like most painters of his time revived the nude as a subject. Look at his *The Birth of Venus*.

Note the contrast between the smooth, curved human forms and the straight trees and harsher surroundings.

Da Vinci, in his portrait *Mona Lisa*, seeks similar values of soft humanity.

Peter Paul Rubens glorified the beauty of the human form in distinctive style and color. In **Venus and Adonis**, note the bulk of the figures.

The man is heavily muscled, the woman weighty although not repugnantly fat. Rubens also used complicated fleshtones, light and dark, to highlight bulk.

Light and dark were used by the late Renaissance Spaniard, El Greco, for dramatic, but not natural, effect.

Here in *View of Toledo* (below), note how light and dark, not variety of color, create the exciting, pre-storm atmosphere.

Courtesy Metropolitan Museum of Art
Bequest of Mrs. H. O. Havemeyer, 1929.
The H.O. Havemeyer Collection.

El Greco and Rubens are classified as Baroque painters.

The next trend in painting after the Baroque was **Rococo** in the 1700s. The delicate, almost fuzzy, lines of Fragonard came after the bold lines and earthy colors of Rubens and El Greco.

Courtesy Metropolitan Museum of Art
Gift of Rene Fribourg, 1953.
Young Woman Reading

Statuary of the Renaissance shows the same tendency toward naturalism and idealism. Look at Della Robbia's *The Adoration* (below).

Courtesy Metropolitan Museum of Art
Bequest of Adele L. Lehman, in memory of Arthur Lehman, 1965.

It is a **terra cotta-relief**. The figures are carved out of a background of clay to be viewed as a picture.

There was a flurry of movements in the 1800s and early 1900s. The most notable was known as realism. It marked the rise of the middle class as a subject of art. The focus is on real life people, poor and moderate, not rich. Some examples include Daumier's **Third Class Carriage** (below)...

Courtesy Metropolitan Museum of Art
The H. O. Havemeyer Collection. Bequest of Mrs. H. O. Havemeyer, 1929.

and Winslow Homer's *The Gulf Stream* (below).

Courtesy the Metropolitan Museum of Art
Wolfe Fund, 1906.

Another example is Magritte's ***The Empire of Light***, a painting of photographic realism.

PRIMITIVE ART

Not to be mistaken as a derogatory label, **primitive art** denotes the fascinating, complex and altogether differently motivated works of the aboriginal, native, and nomadic peoples in Africa, Australia, and the large islands of the southwestern Pacific. It also includes the works of North, Central and South American Indians. Because the Native American population has been largely assimilated or exterminated, much of its art is viewed historically; however, Eskimos and some tribes continue to create in both traditional and modern ways.

Primitive art differs from Western art principally in its motivation. The purpose of Western art since the Renaissance is primarily to be a source of contemplation, appealing to the intellectual powers of the viewer. Primitive art, on the other hand, derives from attempts to worship, protect oneself, and control the supernatural forces of good and evil. Only a few primitive artists have concerned themselves with realism. The range from simplistic beauty to abject horror is represented in statuary, masks, and implements, representing symbols of commerce, magic medicine, and the gods (life, death, fertility, and so on).

Contemporary society recognizes that all human societies merit appreciation and understanding, thus, the study of humanities has been broadened to include the study of primitive art. Primitive art serves as inspiration for modern artists around the world, influencing all societies. Particularly noted is the art of African and Native American cultures. A brief, but not complete, review of their significant achievements follows; read through it, and then spend an hour or two in your local free library looking at a book of photographs of African and North American Indian art. Ask the librarian to recommend some books from the reference section for you to browse. As you do so, try to locate the following list of examples. You will be surprised how quickly you develop the ability to recognize the sources and purposes of primitive art.

AFRICAN ART

African art consists of works produced by the indigenous peoples of the continent, south of the Sahara Desert. Most native African culture was eliminated from North Africa by Islamic invaders more than 1,000 years ago. True African art is highly traditional, mostly with a practical application to religious ceremony. It provides outside observers with insight into the people, their feelings, and their understanding of the forces of the world.

African sculpture has contributed to the development of world art. Modern masters Picasso, Modigliani, and others were influenced by study of African primitive works in the late 19th and early 20th centuries.

Expression of emotion pervades most African artwork. Masks intended to be scary are indeed; beauty, power and other qualities receive similarly strong representation. Detail and craftsmanship prove that the term primitive does not mean "inferior" in relation to African art. This type of art is uniquely African, recognizable not only in materials, such as ivory, but also in characteristically African subjects, such as the people and animals of the continent.

Some important works of African art to recognize and remember:

- **Benin bronzes**. Encountered by a British expedition to western Nigeria in 1897, these bronze castings of masks and heads demonstrate high quality detail and surface finish. The molds were made of wax. Characters represented include average humans, royal personages and mythological figures.

- **Counterweights**. The Ashanti tribe of Ghana and the Baule tribe of the Ivory Coast are two cultures noted for the widespread trade of gold nuggets and dust. They created tiny brass sculptures of humans and animals engaged in everyday tasks, used as counterweights for the gold scales. The figures allude to proverbs and even social satire, demonstrating sophistication. Some critics see an unusual resemblance of the figures, which are not realistic but strangely proportioned, to modern art.

- **Ivory carvings**. Famous from popular literature as a treasure of Africa, ivory carvings were produced from elephant tusks and bones, upon which abstract geometric patterns or commemorative scenes were cut. Their use was primarily in religion, for display around portrait heads such as the Benin bronzes. Ivory was also carved into amulets and figurines with supposed religious powers.

- **Masks**. Ornate, grotesque and highly crafted, masks were produced by various African tribes for use in religious ceremonies. Best known are those of hunting tribes of the Congo (now Zaire), representing the prey to be stalked. The wood-carved masks were worn during ceremonial dances the night before a hunt. They are not realistic; they exaggerate features. Some of the masks use paints, grasses and other natural substances to enhance their impact. Nigerian tribes crafted masks from reeds woven into frames, then covered and modeled with clay.

- **Shrine figures (or fetish figures)**. From statuettes to life-sized representations, shrine figures were created by various African cultures through wood carvings or amalgamations of wood, metal, bone, shell, feather, fur, or other naturally occurring material. Their purpose was either to honor or to ward off the supernatural forces abroad in the world. Worshipped in household shrines, they mimicked human form. They had grotesque shapes and facial expressions.

NATIVE AMERICAN ART

Only recently has society recognized the beauty and value of Native American art, a fascination that has spread throughout Europe and into Asia. The great diversity of tribes is reflected in the diverse art forms practiced.

American Indians descended from many different peoples who emigrated from Asia. They crossed the Alaskan land bridge over thousands of years. They settled in wildly varying climatic zones, achieving differing levels of civilization. Some were nomadic hunters; others were settled farmers. The Indians of American West, notably the Eskimo, Pacific Northwest, Navajo, and Pueblo tribes, still produce their artworks as they did a thousand years ago.

The chief accomplishments of Native Americans were in weaving, pottery, stone and wood carving, beads, and basketry. Some examples to be aware of:

- **Eskimo ivory carvings**. Ancient Eskimos carved walrus tusks into household implements, decorated with fish and animals or geometric patterns. Later Eskimos carved soapstone and wood figures of tundra wildlife, such as bear and caribou.

- **Masks**. Crafted of wood frames and decorated with various natural materials and colorings, North American Indian masks were for spiritual use, usually worn in ceremonies worshipping the gods. Uses and styles varied as widely as the tribes themselves.

- **Pueblos**. Perhaps the first condominium apartments, pueblos were multi-family dwellings created by the tribe of the same name. The buildings were adobe or carved into cliffs. The Pueblos, who lived in the American Southwest, also excelled at pottery.

- **Sand paintings**. These were religious designs mastered by the Navajo of the American Southwest.

- **Weaving**. Also a craft of the Navajo, it included colorful blankets of geometric designs. The so-called "eye of God," popular today as a hanging decoration in American homes, has its artistic roots in Navajo textile craft.

- **Totem poles**. Perhaps the art form most readily associated with North American Indians are totem poles. They are actually the work of tribes of the Pacific Northwest. Placed outside a tribesman's hut, a totem pole explained the rank of the resident within his tribe. They also were used to tell stories out of Native American mythology. They were logs with images of insignia, patron, spirits, mythological characters, "gargoyles" and common animals carved into them and colored.

- **Wampum**. Since the sale of Manhattan Island by the Native Americans to the Dutch, wampum has been mistaken to be North American Indian currency. In reality, it was beads created from seashells, used to decorate apparel. Wampum was produced by the Indians of the area we know now as the northeastern United States and the Canadian province of Quebec.

We have not covered everything there is to know about architecture, sculpture and painting, but you have been exposed to the movements most important to CLEP students. Refer again to the pictures and then try the following sample questions. You should find you have acquired a sense of the styles enabling you to answer many of the examination level questions.

The following artwork refers to Sample Question 1:

Courtesy Metropolitan Museum of Art,
Bequest of Adele L. Lehman, in memory of Arthur Lehman, 1965

1. This special type of sculpture is known as

    (A) portrait
    (B) relief
    (C) religious
    (D) secular
    (E) classical

ANSWER: The correct choice is (B). Relief is a picture carved into stone or clay. Relief is often used in the indoor walls of buildings, particularly churches.

The following artwork refers to Sample Question 2:

2. These structures are examples of

   (A) Greek temples
   (B) naturalism
   (C) Bauhaus buildings
   (D) Egyptian architecture
   (E) prehistoric temples

ANSWER: The correct choice is (D). You can see a pyramid in the background. Pyramids were the architectural development of Egypt. They were used as tombs.

The following artwork refers to Sample Question 3:

3. This representation of the Virgin Mary and Jesus can be described as

(A) romantic
(B) neoclassical
(C) Romanesque
(D) rococo
(E) Byzantine

ANSWER: The correct choice is (E). The stilted postures, dull colors and unrealistic expressions make this icon representative of the Byzantine style of painting.

Taking The CLEP Examination In Humanities

Now that you have finished the entire review section, you are ready to take a short practice test. The test follows the format of the CLEP General Humanities Examination.

It is important that you take this test now. While you may have done well on each type of question in isolation in the preceding section of the book, another skill is necessary. You must practice working with a variety of questions. In effect, you need to practice "switching gears" or training your mind to go from one type of question to another in a short period of time.

Remember, for best results, try to simulate the test situation as nearly as possible. The following procedure should be followed for maximum benefit:

1. Find a quiet spot where you will not be disturbed.

2. Time yourself accurately.

3. Use the separate answer sheet provided to record your answers..

4. Use the coding system to develop a systematic approach to taking the examination.

5. Check you answers.

6. Go back and review.

7. Take the second practice examination.

The following pages are copies* of the actual answer sheet you will use when you take a CLEP examination. The information requested must be filled in so that it can be read by a person and also by a computer. This means on page 1 and 2 of the answer sheet you will blacken the circle which has the same letter or number that appears at the top of that column. When you work in the test section, you will blacken the number you have chosen as the correct answer to the question.

With item Number 8, if you do not know the code number of the institution where you wish to have your scores sent, put four 9's in the spaces provided and indicate the name and address of the school. Enter four 0's if you wish to have your scores sent only to yourself.

It is important for you to understand the answer sheet **before** you go to take the test! Use it when you take your sample test.

SOME TIPS TO REMEMBER WHEN USING A SEPARATE ANSWER SHEET

1. Be **sure** you blacken the entire circle provided for your answer.

2. Be **sure** to put your answers at the proper place on the answer sheet. If you are answering question 30, be **sure** you record your answer at number 30 on the answer sheet.

3. Do **not** put any extra marks on your answer sheet. It may cause the question to be marked incorrect.

4. Be **sure** you record only **one** answer for each question. If you wish to change an answer, be **sure** you erase your first answer completely.

5. Use #2 lead pencils for the multiple choice answers.

COLLEGE-LEVEL EXAMINATION PROGRAM of the College Board
ANSWER SHEET FOR NATIONAL ADMINISTRATIONS — PAGE 1

Use only a soft lead (No. 2) pencil. Be sure each mark is dark and completely fills the intended oval. Erase any errors and stray marks completely.

1. YOUR NAME Omit spaces, hyphens, apostrophes, and Jr. or II.

Last Name — first 12 letters   First Name — first 8 letters   M.I.

2. DATE OF BIRTH

Month	Day	Year
① Jan.		
② Feb.		
③ Mar.		
④ Apr.		
⑤ May		
⑥ Jun.		
⑦ Jul.		
⑧ Aug.		
⑨ Sep.		
⑩ Oct.		
⑪ Nov.		
⑫ Dec.		

3. SEX

Male ①

Female ②

4. SOCIAL SECURITY NUMBER (Optional)

5. CURRENT ENROLLMENT STATUS

① High School
② High School Graduate
③ College Freshman
④ College Sophomore
⑤ College Junior
⑥ College Senior
⑦ College Graduate

6. ETHNIC GROUP (Optional)

How do you describe yourself?

① American Indian, Eskimo or Aleut
② Black, Afro-American or Negro
③ Mexican American or Chicano
④ Oriental or Asian-American
⑤ Puerto Rican-American
⑥ Other Hispanic or Latin American
⑦ White or Caucasian
⑧ Other

7. TEST CENTER CODE NUMBER

Enter the code number in these boxes.

8. SCORE REPORT RECIPIENT

*Enter the Institution Code Number

Blacken the corresponding oval below each box

Institution Name and Location (Print)

Institution Name

City

State

*If you do not have the code number for the institution you want to receive your reports, enter 9999.

9. FEES PAID   See Admission Form.

Examination Fee .... $

Special Administration Fee .... $
(Fee is $10.)

Total Paid ... $

10. TOTAL NUMBER OF EXAMINATIONS YOU ARE GOING TO TAKE AT THIS ADMINISTRATION.

Blacken the corresponding oval below each box. →

○ 1   ○ 4   ○ 7   ○ 10
○ 2   ○ 5   ○ 8   ○ more than 10
○ 3   ○ 6   ○ 9

11. SIGNATURE AND DATE

I accept the conditions set forth in the *Registration Guide* concerning the administration of the tests and reporting of scores.

Today's Date:

DO NOT WRITE IN THIS BOX. FOR ETS USE ONLY.

DO NOT BACK FOLD THIS ANSWER SHEET.

I.N. 202853-185VV127P100

12. YOUR MAILING ADDRESS

Number and Street | **City**

[Bubble grid for letters A–Z and numbers 0–9 for Number and Street, and City fields]

ABBREVIATIONS FOR USE IN STREET ADDRESS

Avenue	AVE	Heights	HTS	Route	RTE
Boulevard	BLVD	Highway	HWY	Second	2ND
Circle	CIR	Mount	MT	South	S
Court	CT	North	N	Southeast	S E
Drive	DR	Northeast	N E	Southwest	S W
East	E	Northwest	N W	Square	SQ
Expressway	EXPWY	Parkway	PKY	Street	ST
First	1ST	Place	PL	Terrace	TER
Fort	FT	Post Office	P O	Third	3RD
Fourth	4TH	Road	RD	West	W

State

01	Alabama	12	Hawaii	23	Michigan	34	North Carolina	45	Utah
02	Alaska	13	Idaho	24	Minnesota	35	North Dakota	46	Vermont
03	Arizona	14	Illinois	25	Mississippi	36	Ohio	47	Virginia
04	Arkansas	15	Indiana	26	Missouri	37	Oklahoma	48	Washington
05	California	16	Iowa	27	Montana	38	Oregon	49	West Virginia
06	Colorado	17	Kansas	28	Nebraska	39	Pennsylvania	50	Wisconsin
07	Connecticut	18	Kentucky	29	Nevada	40	Rhode Island	51	Wyoming
08	Delaware	19	Louisiana	30	New Hampshire	41	South Carolina	52	Puerto Rico
09	Dist. of Col.	20	Maine	31	New Jersey	42	South Dakota	53	Foreign
10	Florida	21	Maryland	32	New Mexico	43	Tennessee		
11	Georgia	22	Massachusetts	33	New York	44	Texas		

U.S. Zip Code

[Bubble grid for numbers 0–9]

Foreign Country Code

[Bubble grid for numbers 0–9]

Your Name (Print): _____
Last   First   M.I.

A. Print

Examination Name: _____ Form Designation: _____

B. TEST CODE

0	0	0	0	0
1	1	1	1	1
2	2	2	2	2
3	3	3	3	3
4	4	4	4	4
5	5	5	5	5
6	6	6	6	6
7	7	7	7	7
8	8	8	8	8
9	9	9	9	9

C. Are you going to take the optional essay portion of this examination?

1 Yes

2 No

D. TEST BOOK SERIAL NUMBER

0	0	0	0	0	0
1	1	1	1	1	1
2	2	2	2	2	2
3	3	3	3	3	3
4	4	4	4	4	4
5	5	5	5	5	5
6	6	6	6	6	6
7	7	7	7	7	7
8	8	8	8	8	8
9	9	9	9	9	9

Be sure each mark is dark and completely fills the intended oval. If you erase, do so completely. You may find more answer responses than you need for one complete 90-minute examination. If so, please leave the extra ovals blank.

1 (A) (B) (C) (D) (E)   31 (A) (B) (C) (D) (E)   61 (A) (B) (C) (D) (E)   91 (A) (B) (C) (D) (E)   121 (A) (B) (C) (D) (E)
2 (A) (B) (C) (D) (E)   32 (A) (B) (C) (D) (E)   62 (A) (B) (C) (D) (E)   92 (A) (B) (C) (D) (E)   122 (A) (B) (C) (D) (E)
3 (A) (B) (C) (D) (E)   33 (A) (B) (C) (D) (E)   63 (A) (B) (C) (D) (E)   93 (A) (B) (C) (D) (E)   123 (A) (B) (C) (D) (E)
4 (A) (B) (C) (D) (E)   34 (A) (B) (C) (D) (E)   64 (A) (B) (C) (D) (E)   94 (A) (B) (C) (D) (E)   124 (A) (B) (C) (D) (E)
5 (A) (B) (C) (D) (E)   35 (A) (B) (C) (D) (E)   65 (A) (B) (C) (D) (E)   95 (A) (B) (C) (D) (E)   125 (A) (B) (C) (D) (E)
6 (A) (B) (C) (D) (E)   36 (A) (B) (C) (D) (E)   66 (A) (B) (C) (D) (E)   96 (A) (B) (C) (D) (E)   126 (A) (B) (C) (D) (E)
7 (A) (B) (C) (D) (E)   37 (A) (B) (C) (D) (E)   67 (A) (B) (C) (D) (E)   97 (A) (B) (C) (D) (E)   127 (A) (B) (C) (D) (E)
8 (A) (B) (C) (D) (E)   38 (A) (B) (C) (D) (E)   68 (A) (B) (C) (D) (E)   98 (A) (B) (C) (D) (E)   128 (A) (B) (C) (D) (E)
9 (A) (B) (C) (D) (E)   39 (A) (B) (C) (D) (E)   69 (A) (B) (C) (D) (E)   99 (A) (B) (C) (D) (E)   129 (A) (B) (C) (D) (E)
10 (A) (B) (C) (D) (E)   40 (A) (B) (C) (D) (E)   70 (A) (B) (C) (D) (E)   100 (A) (B) (C) (D) (E)   130 (A) (B) (C) (D) (E)
11 (A) (B) (C) (D) (E)   41 (A) (B) (C) (D) (E)   71 (A) (B) (C) (D) (E)   101 (A) (B) (C) (D) (E)   131 (A) (B) (C) (D) (E)
12 (A) (B) (C) (D) (E)   42 (A) (B) (C) (D) (E)   72 (A) (B) (C) (D) (E)   102 (A) (B) (C) (D) (E)   132 (A) (B) (C) (D) (E)
13 (A) (B) (C) (D) (E)   43 (A) (B) (C) (D) (E)   73 (A) (B) (C) (D) (E)   103 (A) (B) (C) (D) (E)   133 (A) (B) (C) (D) (E)
14 (A) (B) (C) (D) (E)   44 (A) (B) (C) (D) (E)   74 (A) (B) (C) (D) (E)   104 (A) (B) (C) (D) (E)   134 (A) (B) (C) (D) (E)
15 (A) (B) (C) (D) (E)   45 (A) (B) (C) (D) (E)   75 (A) (B) (C) (D) (E)   105 (A) (B) (C) (D) (E)   135 (A) (B) (C) (D) (E)
16 (A) (B) (C) (D) (E)   46 (A) (B) (C) (D) (E)   76 (A) (B) (C) (D) (E)   106 (A) (B) (C) (D) (E)   136 (A) (B) (C) (D) (E)
17 (A) (B) (C) (D) (E)   47 (A) (B) (C) (D) (E)   77 (A) (B) (C) (D) (E)   107 (A) (B) (C) (D) (E)   137 (A) (B) (C) (D) (E)
18 (A) (B) (C) (D) (E)   48 (A) (B) (C) (D) (E)   78 (A) (B) (C) (D) (E)   108 (A) (B) (C) (D) (E)   138 (A) (B) (C) (D) (E)
19 (A) (B) (C) (D) (E)   49 (A) (B) (C) (D) (E)   79 (A) (B) (C) (D) (E)   109 (A) (B) (C) (D) (E)   139 (A) (B) (C) (D) (E)
20 (A) (B) (C) (D) (E)   50 (A) (B) (C) (D) (E)   80 (A) (B) (C) (D) (E)   110 (A) (B) (C) (D) (E)   140 (A) (B) (C) (D) (E)
21 (A) (B) (C) (D) (E)   51 (A) (B) (C) (D) (E)   81 (A) (B) (C) (D) (E)   111 (A) (B) (C) (D) (E)   141 (A) (B) (C) (D) (E)
22 (A) (B) (C) (D) (E)   52 (A) (B) (C) (D) (E)   82 (A) (B) (C) (D) (E)   112 (A) (B) (C) (D) (E)   142 (A) (B) (C) (D) (E)
23 (A) (B) (C) (D) (E)   53 (A) (B) (C) (D) (E)   83 (A) (B) (C) (D) (E)   113 (A) (B) (C) (D) (E)   143 (A) (B) (C) (D) (E)
24 (A) (B) (C) (D) (E)   54 (A) (B) (C) (D) (E)   84 (A) (B) (C) (D) (E)   114 (A) (B) (C) (D) (E)   144 (A) (B) (C) (D) (E)
25 (A) (B) (C) (D) (E)   55 (A) (B) (C) (D) (E)   85 (A) (B) (C) (D) (E)   115 (A) (B) (C) (D) (E)   145 (A) (B) (C) (D) (E)
26 (A) (B) (C) (D) (E)   56 (A) (B) (C) (D) (E)   86 (A) (B) (C) (D) (E)   116 (A) (B) (C) (D) (E)   146 (A) (B) (C) (D) (E)
27 (A) (B) (C) (D) (E)   57 (A) (B) (C) (D) (E)   87 (A) (B) (C) (D) (E)   117 (A) (B) (C) (D) (E)   147 (A) (B) (C) (D) (E)
28 (A) (B) (C) (D) (E)   58 (A) (B) (C) (D) (E)   88 (A) (B) (C) (D) (E)   118 (A) (B) (C) (D) (E)   148 (A) (B) (C) (D) (E)
29 (A) (B) (C) (D) (E)   59 (A) (B) (C) (D) (E)   89 (A) (B) (C) (D) (E)   119 (A) (B) (C) (D) (E)   149 (A) (B) (C) (D) (E)
30 (A) (B) (C) (D) (E)   60 (A) (B) (C) (D) (E)   90 (A) (B) (C) (D) (E)   120 (A) (B) (C) (D) (E)   150 (A) (B) (C) (D) (E)

DO NOT WRITE IN THESE BOXES.

1R	1W	10	2R	2W	20	3R	3W	30	4R	4W	40	5R	5W	50	6R	6W	60	7R	7W	70	8R	8W	80

9R	9W	90	10R	10W	100	11R	11W	110	12R	12W	120	13R	13W	130	14R	14W	140	15R	15W	150	16R	16W	160

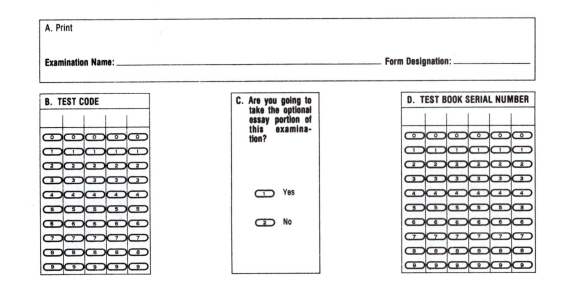

A. Print

Examination Name: _____ Form Designation: _____

B. TEST CODE

C. Are you going to take the optional essay portion of this examination?

⊂1⊃ Yes

⊂2⊃ No

D. TEST BOOK SERIAL NUMBER

Be sure each mark is dark and completely fills the intended oval. If you erase, do so completely. You may find more answer responses than you need for one complete 90-minute examination. If so, please leave the extra ovals blank.

1 Ⓐ Ⓑ Ⓒ Ⓓ Ⓔ	31 Ⓐ Ⓑ Ⓒ Ⓓ Ⓔ	61 Ⓐ Ⓑ Ⓒ Ⓓ Ⓔ	91 Ⓐ Ⓑ Ⓒ Ⓓ Ⓔ	121 Ⓐ Ⓑ Ⓒ Ⓓ Ⓔ
2 Ⓐ Ⓑ Ⓒ Ⓓ Ⓔ	32 Ⓐ Ⓑ Ⓒ Ⓓ Ⓔ	62 Ⓐ Ⓑ Ⓒ Ⓓ Ⓔ	92 Ⓐ Ⓑ Ⓒ Ⓓ Ⓔ	122 Ⓐ Ⓑ Ⓒ Ⓓ Ⓔ
3 Ⓐ Ⓑ Ⓒ Ⓓ Ⓔ	33 Ⓐ Ⓑ Ⓒ Ⓓ Ⓔ	63 Ⓐ Ⓑ Ⓒ Ⓓ Ⓔ	93 Ⓐ Ⓑ Ⓒ Ⓓ Ⓔ	123 Ⓐ Ⓑ Ⓒ Ⓓ Ⓔ
4 Ⓐ Ⓑ Ⓒ Ⓓ Ⓔ	34 Ⓐ Ⓑ Ⓒ Ⓓ Ⓔ	64 Ⓐ Ⓑ Ⓒ Ⓓ Ⓔ	94 Ⓐ Ⓑ Ⓒ Ⓓ Ⓔ	124 Ⓐ Ⓑ Ⓒ Ⓓ Ⓔ
5 Ⓐ Ⓑ Ⓒ Ⓓ Ⓔ	35 Ⓐ Ⓑ Ⓒ Ⓓ Ⓔ	65 Ⓐ Ⓑ Ⓒ Ⓓ Ⓔ	95 Ⓐ Ⓑ Ⓒ Ⓓ Ⓔ	125 Ⓐ Ⓑ Ⓒ Ⓓ Ⓔ
6 Ⓐ Ⓑ Ⓒ Ⓓ Ⓔ	36 Ⓐ Ⓑ Ⓒ Ⓓ Ⓔ	66 Ⓐ Ⓑ Ⓒ Ⓓ Ⓔ	96 Ⓐ Ⓑ Ⓒ Ⓓ Ⓔ	126 Ⓐ Ⓑ Ⓒ Ⓓ Ⓔ
7 Ⓐ Ⓑ Ⓒ Ⓓ Ⓔ	37 Ⓐ Ⓑ Ⓒ Ⓓ Ⓔ	67 Ⓐ Ⓑ Ⓒ Ⓓ Ⓔ	97 Ⓐ Ⓑ Ⓒ Ⓓ Ⓔ	127 Ⓐ Ⓑ Ⓒ Ⓓ Ⓔ
8 Ⓐ Ⓑ Ⓒ Ⓓ Ⓔ	38 Ⓐ Ⓑ Ⓒ Ⓓ Ⓔ	68 Ⓐ Ⓑ Ⓒ Ⓓ Ⓔ	98 Ⓐ Ⓑ Ⓒ Ⓓ Ⓔ	128 Ⓐ Ⓑ Ⓒ Ⓓ Ⓔ
9 Ⓐ Ⓑ Ⓒ Ⓓ Ⓔ	39 Ⓐ Ⓑ Ⓒ Ⓓ Ⓔ	69 Ⓐ Ⓑ Ⓒ Ⓓ Ⓔ	99 Ⓐ Ⓑ Ⓒ Ⓓ Ⓔ	129 Ⓐ Ⓑ Ⓒ Ⓓ Ⓔ
10 Ⓐ Ⓑ Ⓒ Ⓓ Ⓔ	40 Ⓐ Ⓑ Ⓒ Ⓓ Ⓔ	70 Ⓐ Ⓑ Ⓒ Ⓓ Ⓔ	100 Ⓐ Ⓑ Ⓒ Ⓓ Ⓔ	130 Ⓐ Ⓑ Ⓒ Ⓓ Ⓔ
11 Ⓐ Ⓑ Ⓒ Ⓓ Ⓔ	41 Ⓐ Ⓑ Ⓒ Ⓓ Ⓔ	71 Ⓐ Ⓑ Ⓒ Ⓓ Ⓔ	101 Ⓐ Ⓑ Ⓒ Ⓓ Ⓔ	131 Ⓐ Ⓑ Ⓒ Ⓓ Ⓔ
12 Ⓐ Ⓑ Ⓒ Ⓓ Ⓔ	42 Ⓐ Ⓑ Ⓒ Ⓓ Ⓔ	72 Ⓐ Ⓑ Ⓒ Ⓓ Ⓔ	102 Ⓐ Ⓑ Ⓒ Ⓓ Ⓔ	132 Ⓐ Ⓑ Ⓒ Ⓓ Ⓔ
13 Ⓐ Ⓑ Ⓒ Ⓓ Ⓔ	43 Ⓐ Ⓑ Ⓒ Ⓓ Ⓔ	73 Ⓐ Ⓑ Ⓒ Ⓓ Ⓔ	103 Ⓐ Ⓑ Ⓒ Ⓓ Ⓔ	133 Ⓐ Ⓑ Ⓒ Ⓓ Ⓔ
14 Ⓐ Ⓑ Ⓒ Ⓓ Ⓔ	44 Ⓐ Ⓑ Ⓒ Ⓓ Ⓔ	74 Ⓐ Ⓑ Ⓒ Ⓓ Ⓔ	104 Ⓐ Ⓑ Ⓒ Ⓓ Ⓔ	134 Ⓐ Ⓑ Ⓒ Ⓓ Ⓔ
15 Ⓐ Ⓑ Ⓒ Ⓓ Ⓔ	45 Ⓐ Ⓑ Ⓒ Ⓓ Ⓔ	75 Ⓐ Ⓑ Ⓒ Ⓓ Ⓔ	105 Ⓐ Ⓑ Ⓒ Ⓓ Ⓔ	135 Ⓐ Ⓑ Ⓒ Ⓓ Ⓔ
16 Ⓐ Ⓑ Ⓒ Ⓓ Ⓔ	46 Ⓐ Ⓑ Ⓒ Ⓓ Ⓔ	76 Ⓐ Ⓑ Ⓒ Ⓓ Ⓔ	106 Ⓐ Ⓑ Ⓒ Ⓓ Ⓔ	136 Ⓐ Ⓑ Ⓒ Ⓓ Ⓔ
17 Ⓐ Ⓑ Ⓒ Ⓓ Ⓔ	47 Ⓐ Ⓑ Ⓒ Ⓓ Ⓔ	77 Ⓐ Ⓑ Ⓒ Ⓓ Ⓔ	107 Ⓐ Ⓑ Ⓒ Ⓓ Ⓔ	137 Ⓐ Ⓑ Ⓒ Ⓓ Ⓔ
18 Ⓐ Ⓑ Ⓒ Ⓓ Ⓔ	48 Ⓐ Ⓑ Ⓒ Ⓓ Ⓔ	78 Ⓐ Ⓑ Ⓒ Ⓓ Ⓔ	108 Ⓐ Ⓑ Ⓒ Ⓓ Ⓔ	138 Ⓐ Ⓑ Ⓒ Ⓓ Ⓔ
19 Ⓐ Ⓑ Ⓒ Ⓓ Ⓔ	49 Ⓐ Ⓑ Ⓒ Ⓓ Ⓔ	79 Ⓐ Ⓑ Ⓒ Ⓓ Ⓔ	109 Ⓐ Ⓑ Ⓒ Ⓓ Ⓔ	139 Ⓐ Ⓑ Ⓒ Ⓓ Ⓔ
20 Ⓐ Ⓑ Ⓒ Ⓓ Ⓔ	50 Ⓐ Ⓑ Ⓒ Ⓓ Ⓔ	80 Ⓐ Ⓑ Ⓒ Ⓓ Ⓔ	110 Ⓐ Ⓑ Ⓒ Ⓓ Ⓔ	140 Ⓐ Ⓑ Ⓒ Ⓓ Ⓔ
21 Ⓐ Ⓑ Ⓒ Ⓓ Ⓔ	51 Ⓐ Ⓑ Ⓒ Ⓓ Ⓔ	81 Ⓐ Ⓑ Ⓒ Ⓓ Ⓔ	111 Ⓐ Ⓑ Ⓒ Ⓓ Ⓔ	141 Ⓐ Ⓑ Ⓒ Ⓓ Ⓔ
22 Ⓐ Ⓑ Ⓒ Ⓓ Ⓔ	52 Ⓐ Ⓑ Ⓒ Ⓓ Ⓔ	82 Ⓐ Ⓑ Ⓒ Ⓓ Ⓔ	112 Ⓐ Ⓑ Ⓒ Ⓓ Ⓔ	142 Ⓐ Ⓑ Ⓒ Ⓓ Ⓔ
23 Ⓐ Ⓑ Ⓒ Ⓓ Ⓔ	53 Ⓐ Ⓑ Ⓒ Ⓓ Ⓔ	83 Ⓐ Ⓑ Ⓒ Ⓓ Ⓔ	113 Ⓐ Ⓑ Ⓒ Ⓓ Ⓔ	143 Ⓐ Ⓑ Ⓒ Ⓓ Ⓔ
24 Ⓐ Ⓑ Ⓒ Ⓓ Ⓔ	54 Ⓐ Ⓑ Ⓒ Ⓓ Ⓔ	84 Ⓐ Ⓑ Ⓒ Ⓓ Ⓔ	114 Ⓐ Ⓑ Ⓒ Ⓓ Ⓔ	144 Ⓐ Ⓑ Ⓒ Ⓓ Ⓔ
25 Ⓐ Ⓑ Ⓒ Ⓓ Ⓔ	55 Ⓐ Ⓑ Ⓒ Ⓓ Ⓔ	85 Ⓐ Ⓑ Ⓒ Ⓓ Ⓔ	115 Ⓐ Ⓑ Ⓒ Ⓓ Ⓔ	145 Ⓐ Ⓑ Ⓒ Ⓓ Ⓔ
26 Ⓐ Ⓑ Ⓒ Ⓓ Ⓔ	56 Ⓐ Ⓑ Ⓒ Ⓓ Ⓔ	86 Ⓐ Ⓑ Ⓒ Ⓓ Ⓔ	116 Ⓐ Ⓑ Ⓒ Ⓓ Ⓔ	146 Ⓐ Ⓑ Ⓒ Ⓓ Ⓔ
27 Ⓐ Ⓑ Ⓒ Ⓓ Ⓔ	57 Ⓐ Ⓑ Ⓒ Ⓓ Ⓔ	87 Ⓐ Ⓑ Ⓒ Ⓓ Ⓔ	117 Ⓐ Ⓑ Ⓒ Ⓓ Ⓔ	147 Ⓐ Ⓑ Ⓒ Ⓓ Ⓔ
28 Ⓐ Ⓑ Ⓒ Ⓓ Ⓔ	58 Ⓐ Ⓑ Ⓒ Ⓓ Ⓔ	88 Ⓐ Ⓑ Ⓒ Ⓓ Ⓔ	118 Ⓐ Ⓑ Ⓒ Ⓓ Ⓔ	148 Ⓐ Ⓑ Ⓒ Ⓓ Ⓔ
29 Ⓐ Ⓑ Ⓒ Ⓓ Ⓔ	59 Ⓐ Ⓑ Ⓒ Ⓓ Ⓔ	89 Ⓐ Ⓑ Ⓒ Ⓓ Ⓔ	119 Ⓐ Ⓑ Ⓒ Ⓓ Ⓔ	149 Ⓐ Ⓑ Ⓒ Ⓓ Ⓔ
30 Ⓐ Ⓑ Ⓒ Ⓓ Ⓔ	60 Ⓐ Ⓑ Ⓒ Ⓓ Ⓔ	90 Ⓐ Ⓑ Ⓒ Ⓓ Ⓔ	120 Ⓐ Ⓑ Ⓒ Ⓓ Ⓔ	150 Ⓐ Ⓑ Ⓒ Ⓓ Ⓔ

DO NOT WRITE IN THESE BOXES.

1R	1W	10	2R	2W	20	3R	3W	30	4R	4W	40	5R	5W	50	6R	6W	60	7R	7W	70	8R	8W	80

9R	9W	90	10R	10W	100	11R	11W	110	12R	12W	120	13R	13W	130	14R	14W	140	15R	15W	150	16R	16W	160

Sample Examination I

CLEP GENERAL EXAMINATION IN HUMANITIES

SECTION I

TIME: 45 MINUTES   **74 QUESTIONS**

Directions: Each of the questions or incomplete statements is followed by five suggested answers or completions. Select the one that is best in each case.

1. The philosophical attitude of Henry David Thoreau most closely resembles that of

    (A) Mohandas Gandhi and Leo Tolstoy
    (B) Frederich Nietzsche and Aldous Huxley
    (C) Mohandas Gandhi and Aldous Huxley
    (D) John Stuart Mill and René Descartes
    (E) Ralph Waldo Emerson

2. Tom Sawyer, Huckleberry Finn, Jim, and Aunt Polly are creations of what American author?

    (A) Kurt Vonnegut
    (B) William Faulkner
    (C) Henry James
    (D) Mark Twain
    (E) Ring Lardner

3. Of the following plays by William Shakespeare, which is not generally regarded as a history play?

    (A) *Henry the Fourth, Part II*
    (B) *Richard the Second*
    (C) *Julius Caesar*
    (D) *Henry the Eighth*
    (E) *King John*

Questions 4 and 5 refer to the following lines:

> I am the greatest, able to do least,
> Yet most suspected, as the time and place
> Doth make against me, of this direful murder;
> And here I stand, both to impeach and purge
> Myself condemned and myself excused.

4. The passage quoted above is an example of

    (A) metonymy
    (B) simile
    (C) hyperbole
    (D) pathos
    (E) paradox

5. The lines are written in

   (A) iambic tetrameter
   (B) iambic pentameter
   (C) spondee
   (D) dactyllic pentameter
   (E) anapestic tetrameter

6. Actress and singer Judy Garland is probably best known for her role as Dorothy in the film

   (A) *Babes on Broadway*
   (B) *Lullaby on Broadway*
   (C) *The Jazz Singer*
   (D) *The Philadelphia Story*
   (E) *The Wizard of Oz*

7. All of the following are characteristics which qualify *The Aeneid* as an epic except

   (A) heroic symmetry
   (B) epic simile
   (C) invocation of a muse
   (D) *in media res*
   (E) the history of a race

8. The 18th century English poet Alexander Pope was known for his ability to write

   (A) heroic couplet
   (B) dramatic tragedy
   (C) prose fiction
   (D) hymns
   (E) dactyllic verse

9. "The Father of Modern Drama" is generally acknowledged to be

   (A) Edward Albee
   (B) Henrik Ibsen
   (C) August Strindberg
   (D) William Shakespeare
   (E) Samuel Beckett

Questions 10, 11 and 12 refer to the following illustrations (A) through (E):

(A)

Courtesy Metropolitan Museum of Art
Bequest of Adele L. Lehman, in memory of
Arthur Lehman, 1965.

(B)

(C)

Courtesy Metropolitan Museum of Art,
Gift of René Fribourg, 1953.

(D)

(E)

10. Which work is a relief?

    (A)
    (B)
    (C)
    (D)
    (E)

11. Which is in rococo style?

    (A)
    (B)
    (C)
    (D)
    (E)

12. Which is by Leonardo da Vinci?

    (A)
    (B)
    (C)
    (D)
    (E)

13. Which of the following writers were contemporaries?

    (A) Hemingway and Fitzgerald
    (B) Crane and Woolman
    (C) Jonson and Chaucer
    (D) Malory and Pope
    (E) Swift and Orwell

14. In this story, ostensibly for children, a young girl meets such characters as the Mad Hatter, the King and Queen of Hearts and the March Hare. The story is:

    (A) *Gulliver's Travels*
    (B) *Through the Looking Glass*
    (C) *Little Women*
    (D) *Jane Eyre*
    (E) *Alice's Adventures in Wonderland*

15. The author of the work referred to in Question 14 is

    (A) Edgar Allen Poe
    (B) Lewis Carroll
    (C) Laurence Sterne
    (D) Jonathan Swift
    (E) Charlotte Bronte

16. The notion that the size of a man's nose is a clue to his sexual prowess is expressed in

    (A) *Emma*
    (B) *Moll Flanders*
    (C) *The Vicar of Wakefield*
    (D) *Tristram Shandy*
    (E) *Tom Jones*

17. Which of the following composers is NOT Austrian?

    (A) Schubert
    (B) Haydn
    (C) Mozart
    (D) Beethoven
    (E) Bruckner

Questions 18-20 refer to the following lines:

    (A) To be, or not to be= =that is the question:
        Whether 'tis nobler in the mind to suffer
        The slings and arrows of outrageous fortune
        Or to take arms against a sea of troubles
        And by opposing end them.

    (B) Double, double, toil, and trouble,
        Fire burn and cauldron bubble.
        Fillet of fenny snake,
        In the cauldron boil and bake;

87

(C) Hath not a Jew eyes? Hath not a Jew hands, organs dimensions, sense, affections, passions? — fed with the same food, hurt with the same weapons, subject to the same diseases, healed by the same means, warmed and cooled by the same winter and summer as a Christian is?

(D) Wherefore rejoice? What conquest brings he home?
What tributaries follow him to Rome,
To grace in captive bonds his chariot wheels?
You blocks, you stones, you worse than senseless things!
Oh you hard hearts, you cruel men of Rome,
Knew you not Pompey?

(E) Capulet, Montague,
See what a scourge is laid upon your hate,
That heaven finds means to kill your joys with love.

18. Which is from *The Merchant of Venice?*

(A)
(B)
(C)
(D)
(E)

19. Which is from *Hamlet?*

(A)
(B)
(C)
(D)
(E)

20. Which is from *Romeo and Juliet?*

(A)
(B)
(C)
(D)
(E)

21. The "epiphany" of the protagonist is characteristic of the stories of which Irish writer?

(A) Synge
(B) Yeats
(C) O'Casey
(D) Joyce
(E) Swift

22. Which of the following playwrights wrote for "the theater of the absurd?"

    (A) Federico Garcia Lorca
    (B) Anton Chekhov
    (C) Luigi Pirandello
    (D) Thornton Wilder
    (E) Eugene Ionesco

23. A form of poetry derived from the popular song, simple spirited, in short stanzas, in which some story is graphically narrated, is the

    (A) sonnet
    (B) elegy
    (C) roman a'clef
    (D) ballad
    (E) quatrain

Questions 24-26 refer to the following:

> I. *Light in August*
> II. *The Winter of Our Discontent*
> III. *A Farewell to Arms*
> IV. *Of Mice and Men*
> V. *The Old Man and the Sea*

24. Which were written by Ernest Hemingway?

    (A) I, IV, and V
    (B) V only
    (C) I, III and V
    (D) I, II and V
    (E) III and V

25. Which was written by William Faulkner?

    (A) I
    (B) II
    (C) III
    (D) IV
    (E) V

26. Which were written by John Steinbeck?

    (A) IV and V
    (B) III, IV and V
    (C) III and V
    (D) I and II
    (E) II and IV

Question 27 refers to the following passage:

It was a mediocre silent picture with a shopworn theme, and mostly told its story with titles, but it contained three Jolson songs and a snatch of dialogue. That was enough. Once it was released in October 1927, the revolution was underway.

27. The motion picture described above in *The Movies*, by Richard Griffith and Arthur Mayer, is

   (A) *Lullaby on Broadway*
   (B) *The Jazz Singer*
   (C) *I Got Rhythm*
   (D) *The Birth of a Nation*
   (E) *The Vagabond*

28. Which of the following pairs of writers were playwrights?

   (A) Boccaccio and Dante
   (B) Trumbo and Remarque
   (C) Swift and Joyce
   (D) Odets and O'Neill
   (E) Defoe and Roth

29. Which of the pairs of writers mentioned in Question 28 wrote anti-war novels in the early twentieth century?

   (A)
   (B)
   (C)
   (D)
   (E)

30. Which of the writers mentioned in Question 28 were Italian?

   (A)
   (B)
   (C)
   (D)
   (E)

31. The post and lintel was the major architectural contribution of

   (A) ancient Greece
   (B) ancient Egypt
   (C) the Mesopotamians
   (D) the Hittites
   (E) the ancient Romans

32. *Batrachomyomachia*, or *The Battle of the Frogs and the Mice*, is a Greek poem once erroneously attributed to Homer. It describes in Homeric style a battle between the tribe of mice and the frogs, in which such deities as Zeus and Athena take sides. The frogs are at first defeated, but reinforcements finally arrive, in the form of a party of crabs. From the title and plot summary given here, this poem would best be described as

   (A) tragic
   (B) mythic
   (C) mock-heroic
   (D) satiric
   (E) romantic

33. The Latin playwright Plautus reworked an old Greek comedy about lost twin brothers and their reunion into a new play, *The Brothers Menaechmus*. The same plot resurfaces later in literary history, first in Shakespeare and then in a Broadway musical, as

   (A) *All's Well That Ends Well* and *Kiss Me Kate*
   (B) *The Merchant of Venice* and *Mame*
   (C) *The Comedy of Errors* and *The Boys from Syracuse*
   (D) *A Midsummer Night's Dream* and *West Side Story*
   (E) *Loves Labour's Lost* and *Kismet*

34. This author of such famous novels as *Bleak House* and *Our Mutual Friend* began his career with a series of light sketches called the *Pickwick Papers*, under the pseudonym "Boz." He is

   (A) Ernest Hemingway
   (B) Issaac Bickerstaff
   (C) Lemuel Gulliver
   (D) Charles Dickens
   (E) Daniel Defoe

35. "Call me Ishmael" is the opening line of which American novel?

   (A) *Sartoris*
   (B) *The Scarlet Letter*
   (C) *Moby Dick*
   (D) *Portnoy's Complaint*
   (E) *Catch-22*

36. An example of "the tragic flaw" in a literary character is usually thought to be

   (A) Huck Finn's laziness
   (B) Don Quixote's horse
   (C) Kilgore Trout's temper
   (D) Hamlet's indecision
   (E) Oedipus' club foot

37. Of the following, the protagonist and work are correctly paired in

   (A) Squire B, *Pamela*
   (B) Tom Sawyer, *Huckleberry Finn*
   (C) Mordred, *Le Morte D'Arthur*
   (D) Tom Jones, *Moll Flanders*
   (E) Antonio, *The Merchant of Venice*

38. Which novel was <u>not</u> written in the 18th century?

   (A) *Moll Flanders*
   (B) *A Catcher in the Rye*
   (C) *Pamela*
   (D) *The Vicar of Wakefield*
   (E) *Humphry Clinker*

Question 39 refers to the following excerpt:

Her special city was Athens, where her temple, the Parthenon, sat atop the Acropolis. She has no mother, but only a father: Zeus, from whose head she sprang.

39. The Greek goddess described above is

   (A) Pallas Athena
   (B) Hera
   (C) Minerva
   (D) Aphrodite
   (E) Artemis

40. *One Day in the Life of Ivan Denisovich, Cancer Ward* and *A Gulag Archipelago* are novels by what Russian writer?

   (A) Aleksander Solzhenitzyn
   (B) Leonid Brezhnev
   (C) Antoly Dobrynin
   (D) Leo Tolstoy
   (E) Karl Marx

41. An artistic style which deliberately employs irrationality and opposes traditional laws of beauty is

   (A) rococo
   (B) dadaist
   (C) Bauhaus
   (D) baroque
   (E) romantic

42. The author of a story in which a scientist uses dead men's organs to create a new man, and gives him life, is

   (A) T. H. White
   (B) Bram Stoker
   (C) Mary Shelley
   (D) Emily Brontë
   (E) Emily Dickinson

43. *Madame Butterfly*, an early 20th century opera, was written by

   (A) Wolfgang Amadeus Mozart
   (B) Gaetano Donizetti
   (C) Guido D'Arezzo
   (D) Giacomo Puccini
   (E) Giovanni Rigotoni

Questions 44-47 refer to the following lines:

> Some say the world will end in fire,
> Some say in ice.
> From what I've tasted of desire
> I hold with those who favor fire.
> But if I had to perish twice,
> I think I know enough of hate
> To say that for destruction ice
> Is also great
> And would suffice.

44. The rhyme scheme of this poem is

   (A) a-a-b-b-c-d-c-d-e
   (B) a-b-a-b-c-d-c-d-a
   (C) a-b-b-c-c-d-d-e-e
   (D) a-b-a-a-c-d-c-e-c
   (E) a-b-a-a-b-c-b-c-b

45. In this poem, the poet discusses

   (A) two theories for the end of the world
   (B) the cyclical nature of existence
   (C) resurrection
   (D) the poet's tragic flaw
   (E) the hope of mankind

46. The meaning of the poem is enhanced by the poet's use of

   (A) emotion
   (B) learned vocabulary
   (C) understatement
   (D) chiasmus
   (E) onomatopoeia

47. The desire the poet says he has tasted probably

   (A) refreshes
   (B) quenches
   (C) awakens
   (D) depresses
   (E) inflames

Questions 48-50 refer to the following characters:

     I. Romeo
    II. Prospero
   III. Banquo
   IV. Benedick
    V. Falstaff

48.   Which Shakespearean character is the protagonist of a comedy?

    (A)   I
    (B)   II
    (C)   III
    (D)   IV
    (E)   V

49.   Which is the protagonist of a romance?

    (A)   I
    (B)   II
    (C)   III
    (D)   IV
    (E)   V

50.   Which committed suicide?

    (A)   I
    (B)   II
    (C)   III
    (D)   IV
    (E)   V

51.   Agamemmnon's sacrifice of his daughter is told of in

    (A)   *The Iliad*
    (B)   *The Aeneid*
    (C)   *Lycidas*
    (D)   *The Brothers Menaechmus*
    (E)   *The Frogs*

52.   In the Bible, Ishmael was the son of Abraham by Hagar. In literature, then, an "Ishmael" is usually thought of as

    (A)   a poet
    (B)   a seafarer
    (C)   a conquering hero
    (D)   a silly character
    (E)   an outcast

53. The personification of English personal freedom, portrayed by Hogarth and described by Arbuthnot as "an honest plain-dealing fellow, choleric, bold, and of a very inconstant temper," is

(A) Nicholas Frog
(B) Lord Strutt
(C) John Barleycorn
(D) Humphrey Hocus
(E) John Bull

Questions 54-56 refer to the following lines:

The curfew tolls the knell of parting day
The lowing herd wind slowly homeward o'er the lea,
The plowman homeward plods his weary way
And leaves the world to darkness and to me.

54. These lines are from a famous poem by

(A) William Wordsworth
(B) Samuel Johnson
(C) Thomas Gray
(D) Philip Roth
(E) Robert Burns

55. The meter of the poem is

(A) iambic trimeter
(B) octosyllabic diameter
(C) trochaic pentameter
(D) iambic pentameter
(E) anapestic monometer

56. The words "knell," "parting," "lowing," "slowly," "plods," "weary," and "darkness" all help set the tone of this stanza. That tone is best described as

(A) mock-heroic
(B) comic
(C) elegaic
(D) angry
(E) oblique

57. Of these works based on the Arthurian legends, which is by T. H. White?

(A) *Le Morte D'Arthur*
(B) *Camelot*
(C) *The Once and Future King*
(D) *The Idylls of the King*
(E) *The Lady of the Lake*

58. Which is by Sir Thomas Malory?

(A) *Le Morte D'Arthur*
(B) *Camelot*
(C) *The Once and Future King*
(D) *The Idylls of the King*
(E) *The Lady of the Lake*

59. Which is a Broadway musical?

   (A) *Le Morte D'Arthur*
   (B) *Camelot*
   (C) *The Once and Future King*
   (D) *The Idylls of the King*
   (E) *The Lady of the Lake*

60. The opening lines of *The Waste Land*, "April is the cruellest month, breeding/Lilacs out of the dead land, mixing/Memory and desire,/stirring/" are an allusion to

   (A) Homer
   (B) Vergil
   (C) Spenser
   (D) Milton
   (E) Chaucer

61. Structures known as ziggurats would most likely be found in what is today

   (A) Canada
   (B) Russia
   (C) Poland
   (D) Iraq
   (E) East Germany

62. Known for its beautiful representation of the human form in natural posture, the statue *David* was created by

   (A) Boccaccio
   (B) Michelangelo
   (C) an unknown Italian sculptor
   (D) Da Vinci
   (E) Botticelli

Questions 63-65 refer to the following persons:

   I. Johann Sebastian Bach
   II. Johann Gutenberg
   III. Johann Strauss
   IV. Richard Strauss
   V. Richard Wagner

63. Which was the inventor of the printing press?

   (A) I
   (B) II
   (C) III
   (D) IV
   (E) V

64. Which were German composers of opera?

    (A) I and II
    (B) I and V
    (C) III and IV
    (D) IV and V
    (E) I and II

65. Which is famous for his intricate, elaborate compositions for the organ?

    (A) I
    (B) II
    (C) III
    (D) IV
    (E) V

66. The musical instruction *mezzo forte*, abbreviated *mf*, signifies to the performer that the music below it is

    (A) for sopranos only
    (B) for male parts only
    (C) to be played by all instruments
    (D) to be sung moderately soft
    (E) to be sung or played moderately loud

67. Of the following, which is by William Blake?

    (A) *The Four Zoas*
    (B) *Four Sons of Aymon*
    (C) *The Four Horsemen of the Apocalypse*
    (D) *Four Just Men*
    (E) *The Four Georges*

68. An important theme of several poems by William Butler Yeats is

    (A) man's inhumanity to man
    (B) the triumph of technology
    (C) the triumph of reason over emotion
    (D) the emotion of unrequited love
    (E) the transition from mortality to permanence through art

69. In the following pairs of books, which work and its parody are correctly matched?

    (A) *Pamela* and *Shamela*
    (B) *Tom Jones* and *Trom Bones*
    (C) *Young Goodman Brown* and *Joseph Andrews*
    (D) *Moby Dick* and *Billy Budd*
    (E) *Emma* and *Northanger Abbey*

70. All of the following contributed to the development of Gothic architecture, EXCEPT

    (A) growing wealths of cities and towns
    (B) the growing strength of the church
    (C) the Reformation
    (D) increasing trade
    (E) architectural advances

71. A return to stiff, formalized figures, in stilted, unnatural positions, is characteristic of what period of painting?

    (A) Romanesque
    (B) rococo
    (C) baroque
    (D) surrealistic
    (E) Byzantine

72. All of the following are parts of a classical Greek theater, EXCEPT

    (A) orchestra
    (B) proscenium
    (C) paraskenia
    (D) eccyclema
    (E) *deus ex machina* or "God from a machine"

73. The legendary first actor in the Greek theatre was

    (A) Prometheus
    (B) Thespis
    (C) Hector
    (D) Hecuba
    (E) Pericles

74. Peter Bogdanovich, Robert Altman, and Spike Lee are best known for their achievements in

    (A) cinema
    (B) journalism
    (C) theatre
    (D) poetry
    (E) architecture

75. Jealousy is usually thought to be the tragic flaw of the title character in what play by William Shakespeare?

    (A) *Macbeth*
    (B) *Romeo and Juliet*
    (C) *Hamlet*
    (D) *Othello*
    (E) *Richard III*

Questions 76-78 refer to the following types of architecture:

    I. Gothic cathedrals
    II. pyramids
    III. pagodas
    IV. ribbed vaults
    V. frescoes

76. Which was an architectural accomplishment of ancient Egypt?

    (A) I
    (B) II
    (C) III
    (D) IV
    (E) V

77. Which was an architectural contribution of Japan?

    (A) I
    (B) II
    (C) III
    (D) IV
    (E) V

78. Which are paintings on a wall?

    (A) I
    (B) II
    (C) III
    (D) IV
    (E) V

79. *Cosi Fan Tutte*, *Der Rosenkavalier*, and *Aida* are examples of a musical form known as

    (A) opera
    (B) fugue
    (C) commedia dell'arte
    (D) symphonic poem
    (E) folk song

80. What American composer of the 19th century wrote the popular songs "The Old Folks at Home" and "My Old Kentucky Home"?

(A) Robert Louis Stevenson
(B) Wallace Stevens
(C) Stephen Foster
(D) Foster Brooks
(E) Brooks Robinson

Questions 81-84 refer to the following composers:

I. Guido D'Arezzo
II. Antonio Vivaldi
III. George Frederick Handel
IV. Aaron Copland

81. Place the composers in chronological order.

(A) I, II, III, IV
(B) II, III, IV, I
(C) III, I, II, IV
(D) II, I, III, IV
(E) I, II, IV, III

82. Which composer wrote *The Messiah?*

(A) I
(B) II
(C) III
(D) IV
(E) none of the above

83. Which wrote elaborate, religious choral and instrumental music during the Renaissance?

(A) I
(B) II
(C) III
(D) IV
(E) none of the above

84. Which was a monk who first set down the modern method of musical notation?

(A) I
(B) II
(C) III
(D) IV
(E) V

85. Which ancient Greek god is NOT correctly paired with its Roman counterpart?

(A) Ares, Mars
(B) Poseidon, Neptune
(C) Zeus, Jupiter
(D) Hades, Pluto
(E) Hermes, Mars

100

86. The author of *Breakfast of Champions, Slaughterhouse Five,* and *God Bless You, Mrs. Rosewater* is the contemporary American,

    (A) Jacqueline Suzanne
    (B) Mickey Spillane
    (C) Kurt Vonnegut, Jr.
    (D) Angus Black
    (E) Peter Benchley

Questions 87-90 refer to the following musical terms:

    I. clarinets, flutes, bassoons
    II. trumpets, French horns, trombones
    III. violins, violas, cellos
    IV. timpani, celesta, xylophone
    V. chorale, aria, recorder

87. Which group belongs to the woodwind family?

    (A) I
    (B) II
    (C) III
    (D) IV
    (E) V

88. Which group belongs to the brass family?

    (A) I
    (B) II
    (C) III
    (D) IV
    (E) V

89. Which group belongs to the percussion family?

    (A) I
    (B) II
    (C) III
    (D) IV
    (E) V

90. Which group contains instruments found in a string quartet?

    (A) V
    (B) III
    (C) I
    (D) II
    (E) IV

91. The Pulitzer Prize is an award for achievement in

    (A) journalism
    (B) political science
    (C) television
    (D) popular songwriting
    (E) symphonic composition

92. Of the following, which is NOT a playwright?

    (A)   Frings
    (B)   Beckett
    (C)   Albee
    (D)   Schonberg
    (E)   Moliere

93. The ribbed vault, flying buttress, and rosetta window are features of

    (A)   Romanesque tombs
    (B)   Etrurian tombs
    (C)   Etrurian temples
    (D)   medieval European churches
    (E)   Greek temples

94. Which of the following American politicians was also an accomplished architect, as evidenced by Monticello?

    (A)   Calhoun
    (B)   Jefferson
    (C)   Roosevelt
    (D)   Byran
    (E)   Wilson

Question 95 refers to the following excerpt:

"...an age associated with England, in a literary connexion, with the names of Swift, Pope, Defoe, Goldsmith...an age of prose rather than poetry, of lucidity, simplicity, and grace, rational and witty rather than humorous, and somewhat lacking in intensity."

95. The quoted passage states the common misconception about what period of literature?

    (A)   the Victorian period
    (B)   the eighteenth century
    (C)   the restoration
    (D)   the Elizabethan period
    (E)   the romantic period

Questions 96-99 refer to the following lines:

I taste a liquor never brewed = =
From Tankards scooped in Pearl = =
Not all the Vats upon the Rhine
Yield such an Alcohol!

Inebriate of Air = = am I = =   5
And Debauchee of Dew = =
Reeling = = thro endless summer days = =
From inns of Molten Blue = =

When "Landlords" turn the drunken Bee
Out of the Foxglove's door= =   10
When Butterflies = = renounce their "drams" = =
I shall but drink the more!

Till Seraphs swing their snowy Hats = =
And Saints = = to windows run = =
To see the little Tippler   15
Leaning against the = = Sun = =

96. The "inns of molten blue" in line 8 are

   (A)   oceans
   (B)   lakes
   (C)   skies
   (D)   candle wax
   (E)   country inns

97. The "little Tippler" of line 16 is

   (A)   the pastor
   (B)   the bee
   (C)   the butterfly
   (D)   the poet
   (E)   the brewmaster

98. The poem is similar in theme to

   (A)   those of other American and English romantics
   (B)   *The Waste Land*
   (C)   medieval miracle plays
   (D)   *Paradise Lost*
   (E)   *The Essay on Man*

99. This poem was probably written by

   (A)   Edgar Allen Poe
   (B)   Edwin Arlington Robinson
   (C)   Marianne Moore
   (D)   Emily Dickinson
   (E)   Simon and Garfunkel

100. An icon is

 (A) an eight-line poem, written in alternating lines of iambic pentameter and iambic trimeter
 (B) geometric shapes reproduced on leather by means of lithography
 (C) a wood-cut
 (D) a religious image painted on a wooden panel
 (E) a medieval religious chant written in monophony

101. Which of the following is NOT known for his paintings?

 (A) Fragonard
 (B) Dali
 (C) Picasso
 (D) Segovia
 (E) El Greco

102. The "international style" is a type of symphonic music produced in

 (A) Europe
 (B) the 20th century
 (C) New York City
 (D) the Middle Ages
 (E) Hitler's Germany

103. Which of the following motion pictures did NOT win an Academy award for best picture of the year in which it was produced?

 (A) *Fiddler on the Roof*
 (B) *The French Connection*
 (C) *Oliver*
 (D) *The Godfather*
 (E) *The Sound of Music*

104. O. Henry's short story "The Gift of the Magi" and Sophocles' *Oedipus the King* have in common

 (A) leading characters of the same name
 (B) a setting in Greece
 (C) no female characters
 (D) irony
 (E) a Christian denouement

105. Orson Welles' thinly disguised portrayal of William Randolph Hearst came in the movie

 (A) *Casablanca*
 (B) *Citizen Kane*
 (C) *A Sainted Devil*
 (D) *The Thin Man*
 (E) *San Francisco*

106. The killing of an albatross by a sailor brings death to all others on his boat, but eventually leads to the sailor's spiritual rebirth in

   (A) Synge's *Riders to the Sea*
   (B) Strindberg's *The Dream Play*
   (C) Wolfe's *Look Homeward, Angel*
   (D) Melville's *Billy Budd*
   (E) Coleridge's *The Rime of the Ancient Mariner*

107. Bilbo Baggins, an imaginary creature called a hobbit, was created by

   (A) C. S. Lewis
   (B) Randall Jarrell
   (C) E. B. White
   (D) T. S. Eliot
   (E) J. R. R. Tolkien

108. *All the President's Men*, a book synthesizing the investigative reporting efforts of two Washington Post journalists, details the events leading up to the resignation of president Richard Nixon. Its co-authors are

   (A) Carl Bernstein and Bob Woodward
   (B) William Randolph Hearst and Joseph Pulitzer
   (C) Samuel Johnson and James Boswell
   (D) Bob Barlett and James Steele
   (E) Theodore White and Benjamin Bradlee

Questions 109-111 refer to the following works of art:

   I.   "The Thinker"
   II. "Whistler's Mother"
   III. "The Third Class Carriage"
   IV. "Water Lilies"
   V.   "The Night Watch"

109. Which is by Rembrandt?

   (A) I
   (B) II
   (C) III
   (D) IV
   (E) V

110. Which is (are) sculpture?

   (A) I
   (B) II and IV only
   (C) V
   (D) I and V only
   (E) I, III and V

111. Which represents realism in painting?

(A) II
(B) III
(C) IV
(D) I
(E) V

112. Sherlock Holmes, a detective often assisted by his friend, Dr. Watson, is the fictional creation of which English writer?

(A) Arthur Conan Doyle
(B) W. H. Auden
(C) Lord Byron
(D) Kenneth Clarke
(E) Orlando Gibbons

113. A madrigal is

(A) four string instruments playing in unison
(B) four sets of eighth notes
(C) a four-part tonal poem
(D) four piano sonatas
(E) four-part vocal song, from the Middle Ages

114. A modern Broadway musical based on Cervantes' *Don Quixote* is

(A) *Man of La Mancha*
(B) *Man and Superman*
(C) *A Man for All Seasons*
(D) *The Wild Duck*
(E) *Les Miserables*

Questions 115-117 refer to the following lines:

> Whan that Aprille with shoures soote
> The droghte of March hath perced to the roote,
> And bathed every veyne in swich licour,
> Of which vertu engendred is the flour;

115. The passage above is written in

(A) Middle English
(B) Old English
(C) Trochaic
(D) blank verse
(E) sprung rhythm

116. "Droghte" in line 2 means

(A) drug
(B) season
(C) cold
(D) dryness
(E) paucity

117. The season described is

   (A) midsummer
   (B) spring
   (C) fall
   (D) early winter
   (E) late winter

Questions 118-119 refer to the following excerpt:

"For unto us a child is born, and his name shall be called Wonderful Counsellor, Almighty God, the Everlasting Father, the Prince of Peace."

118. The preceding text from Isaiah provided the inspiration for a grand chorus in an oratorio by

   (A) George Friderick Handel
   (B) Oscar Hammerstein
   (C) Matthew Dubourg
   (D) Giovanni Conforti
   (E) Dmitri Borisovich Kabalevsky

119. The work referred to above may best be described as

   (A) rococo
   (B) baroque
   (C) Renaissance
   (D) grand choeur
   (E) international style

120. Another composer of the same stylistic period is

   (A) Vivaldi
   (B) Beethoven
   (C) Bach
   (D) Rimsky-Korsakov
   (E) Rebikov

Questions 121-123 refer to the following pieces of literature:

   I. *De Rerum Natura*
   II. *Huckleberry Finn*
   III. *The Rape of the Lock*
   IV. *Tristram Shandy*
   V. *Titus Andronicus*

121. Which is a mock-epic?

   (A) I
   (B) II
   (C) III
   (D) IV
   (E) V

122. Which is non-fictional didactic literature?

    (A)   I
    (B)   II
    (C)   III
    (D)   IV
    (E)   V

123. Which is by Laurence Sterne?

    (A)   I
    (B)   II
    (C)   III
    (D)   IV
    (E)   V

Questions 124-125 refer to the following painting:

124. The persons depicted in the illustration on the preceding page are

    (A) Miriam and Moses
    (B) Abraham and Isaac
    (C) Ruth and Naomi
    (D) Mary and Jesus
    (E) Elizah and Elisha

125. The style is

    (A) rococo
    (B) Byzantine
    (C) baroque
    (D) Renaissance
    (E) Roman revival

126. The portion of a story that relates background information on characters and setting is referred to as

    (A) denouement
    (B) credenza
    (C) *in media res*
    (D) *deus ex machina*
    (E) exposition

127. Which of the following is classified as a "metaphysical" poet?

    (A) McKuen
    (B) Donne
    (C) Malory
    (D) Ferlinghetti
    (E) Cicero

128. Which pair of poets best reflects the notion that "whoever degrades another degrades me, and whatever is done or said returns at last to me"?

    (A) Walt Whitman and John Donne
    (B) Marianne Morre and T. S. Eliot
    (C) Rudyard Kipling and Robert Frost
    (D) Vergil and John Milton
    (E) Emily Dickinson and Alexander Pope

129. Music marked *legato* should be played

    (A) loudly
    (B) softly
    (C) smoothly
    (D) vigorously
    (E) slowly

130. Other than the vertical bar at its left end, what is the first musical symbol to appear on a staff?

(A) time signature
(B) measure
(C) half note
(D) key signature
(E) clef

Questions 131-135 refer to the following musical compositions:

    I. *Romeo and Juliet* by Prokofiev
    II. *Romeo and Juliet* by Tchaikovsky
    III. "Every valley shall be exalted..." by Handel
    IV. Beethoven's Ninth Symphony
    V. *The Magic Flute* by Mozart

131. Which is an aria?

(A) I
(B) II
(C) III
(D) IV
(E) V

132. Which is the score for a ballet?

(A) I
(B) II
(C) III
(D) IV
(E) V

133. Which is an opera?

(A) I
(B) II
(C) III
(D) IV
(E) V

134. Which is an overture-fantasia?

(A) I
(B) II
(C) III
(D) IV
(E) V

135. Which is also known as "Choral"?

(A) I
(B) II
(C) III
(D) IV
(E) V

136. Yellow bile, black bile, blood, and phlegm, which Renaissance writers thought affected personalities, are known as

    (A) the four humors
    (B) the four horsemen
    (C) the good humors
    (D) the good elements
    (E) the tri-elements

137. Which cannot have been source material for Shakespeare's plays?

    (A) *The Decameron* by Boccaccio
    (B) commedia dell'arte
    (C) *Metamorphoses* by Ovid
    (D) *Paradise Lost* by Milton
    (E) *The Annals of Imperial* Rome by Tacitus

138. A character described as a sycophant, for example, Phormio from *Phormio* or Mosca from *Volpone*, is

    (A) a pedant
    (B) a tyrant
    (C) a parasite
    (D) a despot
    (E) a braggart

139. Counterpoint is an essential part of what musical form?

    (A) aria
    (B) duple time
    (C) cassation
    (D) doppio movimento
    (E) fugue

140. An 18th century English painter whose works criticized and satirized his society, while especially ridiculing the French, was

    (A) William Hogarth
    (B) Orlando Gibbons
    (C) Michael Pacher
    (D) Mathias Grunewald
    (E) Norman Rockwell

141. The function of mausoleums, pyramids, and sarcophagi is related to

    (A) burial
    (B) marriage
    (C) eating
    (D) farming
    (E) geometry

142. Gauguin and Van Gogh were founders of what artistic movement?

(A) Cinquecento
(B) Expressionism
(C) Art Deco
(D) Romanticism
(E) Realism

Questions 143-144 refer to the following art styles:

I. rococo
II. baroque
III. realistic
IV. Renaissance

143. The correct chronological order of the styles above is

(A) I, II, III, IV
(B) II, I, III, IV
(C) IV, I, II, III
(D) IV, II, I, III
(E) IV, III, II, I

144. Which style is characterized by the paintings of Peter Paul Rubens?

(A) I
(B) II
(C) III
(D) IV
(E) none of the above

145. The most well-known and accepted reference work dealing with the etymology and meanings of words is

(A) *The Random House Dictionary*
(B) *The Columbia Desk Reference Encyclopedia*
(C) *Dr. Johnson's Dictionary*
(D) *The Oxford English Dictionary*
(E) *The Dictionary of National Biography*

> Dull sublunary lovers' love
> (Whose soul is sense) cannot admit
> Absence, because it does remove
> Those things which elemented it.

146. In line one, "sublunary" means

    (A) science fictional
    (B) philosophical
    (C) denigrating
    (D) romantic
    (E) earthly

147. In line two, "sense" means

    (A) sensuality
    (B) common sense
    (C) right person
    (D) the great chain of being
    (E) spirit

148. In line four, "elemented" means

    (A) analyzed
    (B) fell out of
    (C) learned
    (D) hated
    (E) constituted

149. One literary technique exemplified in this poem is

    (A) end-stopping
    (B) "throwing"
    (C) the writing of couplets
    (D) enjambement
    (E) allusion

150. This poem's title is "A Valediction: Forbidding Mourning," and it is by John Donne. It contains the most famous of Donne's metaphysical concepts about

    (A) an apple in the Garden of Eden
    (B) a compass
    (C) a ziggurat
    (D) a mosaic
    (E) a chain

ANSWERS AND EXPLANATIONS

SAMPLE EXAMINATION I

SECTION I

1. **(A)** Thoreau's essay "On the Duty of Civil Disobedience" explains his belief in passive resistance to questionable laws when those laws are enforced by coercion. Gandhi in India and Tolstoy in eastern Europe advocated this stand.

2. **(D)** All are characters from Twain's Huckleberry Finn. Tom, Huck, and Aunt Polly also appear in Twain's *Tom Sawyer*.

3. **(C)** Julius Caesar is generally regarded as a tragedy rather than a history because it does not deal with the history of the English kings. All the others do.

4. **(E)** All these statements by Friar Laurence in *Romeo and Juliet*, while appearing self-contradictory to the other characters, are actually true. Therefore, the best answer is paradox. None of the statements involves comparison, thus (A) and (B) are eliminated. There is no exaggeration, so (C) cannot be correct. While the entire play is one of emotion, and while Laurence is a pathetic character, the quoted passage is insufficient as an example of pathos.

5. **(B)** The lines have five two-syllable feet in each, with the accent on the second syllable. For example, the first line diagrammed looks like this:

   ᴗ′ ᴗ ′ ᴗ ′ᴗ ′ᴗ ′
   I am/the great/est, a/ble to/do least,

6. **(E)** Although Garland appeared with Mickey Rooney in *Babes on Broadway*, that movie does not approach the artistic or commercial success of *The Wizard of Oz*. *The Jazz Singer* was the first "talkie" and starred Al Jolson.

7. **(A)** There is no acknowledged characteristic of epic literature called "heroic symmetry." All the other choices are bona fide epic characteristics applicable to *The Aeneid*.

8. **(A)** Heroic couplet, or rhymed iambic pentameter verse, is a trademark of Pope.

9. **(B)** Ibsen is so named because he first brought realism to the stage in such plays as *A Doll's House* and *Ghosts*. His plays enjoy much popularity today for their timeliness and timelessness (*A Doll's House* and *Hedda Gabler* deal with the role of women in society; *Ghosts* involves venereal disease). Strindberg, a contemporary of Ibsen, wrote naturalistic and symbolic plays. Albee is a 20th century playwright. Beckett's plays are for the theater of the absurd.

10. **(B)** A relief is a picture carved in stone or clay. It is usually found in the walls of buildings, but is also seen on tombstones and columns.

11. **(D)** Rococo painting is marked by delicate colors and light, fuzzy lines, as here in Fragonard's "A Young Woman Reading".

12. **(C)** This, of course, is da Vinci's famous "Mona Lisa."

13. (A) Both Hemingway and Fitzgerald wrote during the early decades of the 20th century.

14. (E) *Alice's Adventures in Wonderland* is said to be quoted more often than any other work except the Bible and Shakespeare. (B) is the sequel to (E).

15. (B) Lewis Carroll is also known by his actual name, Charles Dodgson.

16. (D) The idea is expressed by Tristram's father.

17. (D) Beethoven was a German.

18. (C) Shylock, the antagonist, makes this moving prose speech.

19. (A) Of all the passages of Shakespeare, this may be the best known. It is Hamlet's most famous soliloquy.

20. (E) Capulet and Montague are the feuding families in *Romeo and Juliet*. Of the remaining choices, (B) is the chant of the witches in *Macbeth*, and (D) is Marullus' speech decrying the Roman welcome for Caesar from *Julius Caesar*.

21. (D) The device is best seen in *Dubliners*, a collection of short stories by James Joyce.

22. (E) Ionesco, a French playwright, is the correct answer. An example of his absurdity for the stage is a one-act play called *The Lesson*. All the others wrote for the traditional stage.

23. (D) Only (D) is a possible answer.

24. (E)

25. (A)

26. (E)

27. (B)

28. (D) Odets and O'Neill both wrote for the 20th century American theater. Of the others, Boccaccio and Dante were Italian poets of the late Middle Ages; Trumbo and Remarque wrote anti-war novels following World War I; Swift and Joyce were Irish writers of different periods; Defoe was an 18th century English writer of early novels, while Roth is a 20th century American novelist.

29. (B) (see explanation for question 28)

30. (A) (see explanation for question 28)

31. (A) The ancient Egyptians contributed the pyramids, the Mesopotamians ziggurats, and the ancient Romans the semi-circular arch. The Hittites made no contribution to architecture.

32. (C) Since the question tells the reader the poem is written in Homeric style, he knows that the poem must be in epic style. However, since the characters are nonsensical (frogs and mice), he must also know that the poem makes fun of heroic style. While it probably could be described as satiric, such a poem is best described as mock-heroic.

33. (C)

34. (D)

35. (C)

36. (D) Tragic flaw is usually thought to be that trait of a character which ultimately leads to his downfall or death in a story. Hamlet's inability to act decisively following the murder of his father is his tragic flaw. Merely a boy, Huck cannot be judged for his laziness, if indeed it can be shown he was lazy; in any case, Huck is not a tragic character. Don Quixote's horse is not a trait of Quixote, so (B) would be a nonsensical choice. Kilgore Trout is an even-tempered man in Vonnegut's books; (C) is incorrect. Oedipus' club foot never hindered him as a prince or king, so (E) is wrong.

37. (E) Antonio is the main character with whom the reader identifies, and for whom the reader "roots." Squire B is the antagonist of *Pamela*. While Tom Sawyer makes occasional appearances in *Huckleberry Finn*, he is not the protagonist. Tom Jones is the protagonist of *Tom Jones*, not *Moll Flanders*. Mordred is the antagonist of *Le Morte D'Arthur*.

38. (B) *A Catcher in the Rye* was written by J. D. Salinger in the 20th century. All the others are English works, usually held to be novels, of the 18th century .

39. (A) This is undoubtedly Pallas Athena. Minerva ruled practically the same domain, but was a Roman goddess. Hera's realm was that of marriage and married women. Aphrodite was the goddess of love and beauty. Artemis was the protector of wild things.

40. (A) Solzhenitsyn's other famous books include *Cancer Ward, August 1914* and the recent *A Gulag Archipelago*. Brezhnev and Dobrynin were Soviet politicians. Tolstoy, who lived during the 19th and early 20th centuries before the Communist takeover in Russia, wrote the huge novel *War and Peace*. Marx, along with Lenin an innovator of Soviet Communism, wrote largely philosophical works.

41. (B) Dadaism reached its peak early in the 20th century between the world wars. Bauhaus art incorporates the functional aspect of things, particularly in architecture, but is not thought to intentionally exclude beauty from its modernistic appearance. Rococo, baroque, and romantic art always sought beauty as a characteristic.

42. (C) The book was *Frankenstein*, which bears little resemblance to the movie of the same name. Stoker wrote *Dracula*.

43. (D) Puccini wrote the opera, whose main character was Benjamin Franklin Pinkerton. Guido d'Arezzo was the monk who invented our modern system of musical notation.

44. (E) To figure out a rhyme scheme of a poem, assign, alphabetically, a letter for each new rhyme sound at the end of each line.

45. (A) Only (A) is a logical choice.

46. (C) For such an important event, the understatement and simplicity heighten the meaning.

47. (E) No choice, but this is similar in meaning to the statement, which is made in lines three and four.

48. (D) Benedick appears in *Much Ado About Nothing*.

49.   (B)   Prospero is from *The Tempest*.

50.   (A)   Romeo, seeing the apparently dead Juliet, kills himself in *Romeo and Juliet*.

51.   (A)   Agamemnon, general of the united Greek armies against Troy, sacrifices Iphigenia in Homer's epic. *The Aeneid* tells of Aeneas' flight from Troy, wanderings in the Mediterranean area, and founding of the Roman race. "Lycidas," written correctly in quotation marks because it is a short poem, is a pastoral elegy by John Milton in memory of one of his schoolmates.

              The Brothers Menaechmus is Plautus' play about two sets of long-lost brothers. *The Frogs*, a satirical play on the gods, was written by Aristophanes, a Greek dramatist.

52.   (E)   Considering the Bible stories about Ishmael in Genesis, only (E) is logical.

53.   (E)

54.   (C)   The poem is "Elegy Written in a Country Churchyard," commonly known as Gray's elegy.

55.   (D)   Only (D) is a logical answer. (B) is not a recognized meter.

56.   (C)   Not only is (C) the best description of the tone, but also none of the other choices could logically describe it.

57.   (C)   White wrote *The Once and Future King*, sometimes referred to as a children's book. Thomas Malory wrote (A); (B) is a Broadway musical based on White's book; (D) is by Alfred Lord Tennyson.

58   (A)   (see explanation for question 57)

59   (B)   (see explanation for question 57)

60.   (E)   Chaucer's *Canterbury Tales* begins with the same subject but from the opposite point of view. Also, Chaucer's work is written in Middle English.

61.   (D)   Ziggurats are pyramid-like structures built by ancient Mesopotamians.

62.   (B)

63.   (B)

64.   (D)

65.   (A)

66.   (E)   "*mf*" is one of several such abbreviated instructions. "*mp*," or *mezzo piano*, means moderately soft. "*p*" and "*f*" mean soft and loud, respectively, while "*pp*" and "*ff*" mean very soft and very loud, respectively.

67.   (A)   Only *The Four Zoas* was written by Blake.

68.   (E)   Several of Yeats' best and most important poems deal with the author's search for immortality through art. "Sailing to Byzantium" is one poem that clearly expounds the theme. None of the other choices in question 68 is a major Yeats theme.

69. (A) *Pamela*, one of the earliest novels, was written in the 18th century by Samuel Richardson. Dealing with a pretty but poor girl who is put out to be a servant, and who defends her honor from a sexually aggressive master, *Pamela* inspired a parody by Henry Fielding brazenly entitled *Shamela*. The fact that Pamela agrees to a physical relationship with her master after he ultimately marries her caused Fielding to assert that her actions are nothing less than prostitution. Among the other choices, (B) matches *Tom Jones* by Fielding with a fictional title of a non-existent book; (C) pairs Nathaniel Hawthorne's short story "Young Goodman Brown" (correctly placed in quotes) with another *Pamela* parody by Fielding, *Joseph Andrews*; (D) contains two works by Herman Melville; and (E) contains two works by Jane Austen.

70. (C) The Reformation was a deterrent to the accumulation of wealth and power by the Roman Catholic church, which inspired and permitted construction of great Gothic cathedrals. The reformation opposed some of the spiritual implications of the style.

71. (E) The question is a good definition of Byzantine painting. Such painting was usually upon wood, the resulting images called icons.

72. (B) The proscenium, or picture-frame stage, appeared after the Middle Ages.

73. (B) Thespis gives his name to the acting profession, members of which are called thespians. Prometheus (A) was a Greek god. Hector (C) was a heroic warrior of Troy. Hecuba (D) was a wife of the Trojan king, Priam. Pericles ruled Athens during the so-called Golden Age of Greece.

74. (A) All three have directed movies of popular and critical acclaim (Bogdanovich: *What's Up, Doc?* and *Paper Moon*. Altman: *Nashville* and *A Wedding*. Lee: *Boyz N The Hood* and *X*.).

SECTION 2

75. (D) It is jealousy, planted in his mind by Iago, that prompts Othello to murder his wife, Desdemona. When Othello learns the rashness of his action, he commits suicide.

76. (B) Pyramids served as mausoleums for Egyptian pharaohs.

77. (C) Pagodas originally served as temples.

78. (E) Perhaps the most famous fresco is painted on the ceiling of the Sistine Chapel in Rome. It contains scenes from the Bible, and was painted by Michelangelo.

79. (A) Mozart created the first, Richard Strauss the second and Verdi the third.

80. (C) Foster is the only composer out of the five choices.

81. (A) D'Arezzo lived during the late 10th and early 11th centuries, and devised the system of musical notation very similar to the one in use today. Vivaldi (c. 1675-1741) was an Italian violinist and composer. Handel (1675-1759), while German, lived in England much of the time and was very popular there. Among the multitude of compositions of various types that Handel wrote, the oratorio *Messiah* and orchestral composition *Water Music* are best known. Aaron Copland, American composer of *Appalachian Spring*, was born in 1900 and died in 1992.

82. (C)

83.	(B)	
84.	(A)	
85.	(E)	Hermes, the messenger of Zeus, was renamed Mercury in the Roman system. Mars, the Roman god of war is correctly matched with his Greek counterpart, Ares, in (A).
86.	(C)	
87.	(A)	
88.	(B)	
89.	(D)	
90.	(B)	
91.	(A)	The award is named after Joseph Pulitzer, a St. Louis newspaper publisher of the early 20th century who became rich and set up the Pulitzer Foundation, which makes the awards. Ironically, the funds came from his profits from a chain of "yellow" papers.
92.	(D)	Schönberg is a composer.
93.	(D)	All are essential elements of Gothic architecture.
94.	(B)	Thomas Jefferson epitomized the "Renaissance man" who can do every task himself. The Virginian was a noted architect, political scientist, agriculturist, inventor, musician, and lexicographer.
95.	(B)	Swift, Pope, Defoe and Goldsmith all wrote during the 18th century in England, hence the obvious answer is (B). The misconception concerns the lack of good poetry and humor.
96.	(C)	The imagery in these lines is of clear, blue summer days.
97.	(D)	The little tippler is a reference to line 12, in which the poet says "I shall but drink the more."
98.	(A)	No other choice would reflect the themes of the poem.
99.	(D)	Keys to recognizing Dickinson's poems include the concise, succinct vocabulary and unusual punctuation employing dashes.
100.	(D)	Only (D) is a logical choice. The others are entirely fictional.
101.	(D)	Andres Segovia was best known for his skill in playing the classical guitar.
102.	(B)	It is a 20th century form produced around the world.
103.	(A)	
104.	(D)	The plots and themes of both works indispensably employ irony.
105.	(B)	
106.	(E)	
107.	(E)	Bilbo Baggins is the central character of Tolkien's book, *The Hobbit*.
108.	(A)	Bernstein and Woodward have been credited with uncovering the Watergate scandal through their dogged investigation of the bugging and break-in of Democratic National Headquarters in 1972.

109. (E) "The Night Watch" uses glints of light in contrast with dark tones and shadows to achieve great effect.

110. (A) "The Thinker" is by Rodin.

111. (B) This painting by Daumier is considered representative of the movement called realism, which attempted to capture everyday people in everyday activities.

112. (A) Arthur Conan Doyle's accounts of his world travels were also widely read, in books and newspapers.

113. (E) Originally, the madrigal was a poem sung by a soprano, an alto, a tenor and a bass.

114. (A) *Man of La Mancha*, while taking many liberties, is a generally faithful synthesis of the Quixote stories.

115. (A) Middle English is a language largely understandable by modern English-speaking readers, whereas Old English is not. None of the metrical choices in (C), (D), and (E) applies.

116. (D) In modern English, "droghte" would be read "drought."

117. (B) April showers and flowers? Definitely, spring is described.

118. (A) "For unto us a child is born..." is a chorus from *Messiah* by Handel.

119. (B) Baroque music and architecture both used lavish decoration.

120. (C) Bach was another Baroque composer, noted chiefly for his organ compositions.

121. (C) Pope's poem, with gods, battles, mythology and epic simile, makes a mountain out of a mole hill. The story so told concerns a suitor who cuts a lock of a beautiful woman's hair without her permission.

122. (A) This work by Lucretius teaches the reader about Epicurean philosophy.

123. (D) *Tristram Shandy*, a thick volume rated as one of the best and funniest books in English, is by Sterne.

124. (D) Note the holy halos that are given only to the members of Christ's family and heavenly beings in painting.

125. (B)

126. (E) Exposition usually comes at the beginning of a story, play, or book, and always gives the information necessary for the reader or audience to understand the setting and characters.

127. (B)

128. (A) In their works, many decades and oceans apart, Whitman and Donne expound the metaphysical notion that humanity is injured by the bad actions of each person, and conversely, that it is helped by the good actions of each.

129. (C) *Legato* is an Italian word, as are most musical instructions in notation. To be played loudly or softly, music should be marked "*forte*" or "*piano*," respectively. "*Lento*" means slowly, while "*allegro*" means vigorously or lively.

130. (E)

131. (C) "Every valley shall be exalted..." is a tenor aria from *Messiah*, Part the First.

132. (A)

133. (E)

134. (B)

135. (D) The Ninth Symphony is subtitled "Choral."

136. (A) Medieval thought, without the benefit of modern chemistry, held that the body was composed of four elements: fire, air, water and earth. The relative amounts of each controlled a person's production of the four humors, which in turn colored personalities, the old scholars believed.

137. (D) Since it was written years after Shakespeare's death, *Paradise Lost* could not have been a source of Shakespearean plots. All the others could have been, and probably were.

138. (C) The hanger-on, a disgusting person who would flatter a rich man, serve as a yes-person and testify falsely for pay in court, is a sycophant.

139. (E) By their nature, fugues require contrapuntal melodies. Counterpoint has no relationship whatsoever to the other choices in this question.

140. (A) Hogarth's paintings are rich, useful and funny representation of 18th century England. Rockwell (E) was an American painter of the 20th century. Gibbons was an English composer of the late 1500s and early 1600s.

141. (A) While various types of art may decorate these structures and creations, their function is for the burial of the dead.

142. (B)

143. (D) Whether painting, sculpture, architecture or music, the progression is the same.

144. (B) Rubens' paintings were characterized by full-figured people and bold, contrasting colors.

145. (D)

146. (E) Sublunary, literally "beneath the moon," means earthly.

147. (A) In this context, sense must mean sensuality. When the lovers are apart, they cannot engage in the sensual activities that constituted their love to begin with.

148. (E) The elements are the basic building blocks of matter. Hence, elemented means constituted.

149. (D)

150. (B) Some knowledge of this famous poem is required to answer this question. Such questions appear on the CLEP humanities examinations, but usually deal only with very well known works such as "A Valediction: Forbidding Mourning."

Now that you have corrected Test I, review your areas of weakness and take Test II.

Sample Examination II

CLEP GENERAL EXAMINATION IN HUMANITIES

SECTION I

TIME: 45 MINUTES   **81 QUESTIONS**

Directions: Each of the questions or incomplete statements is followed by five suggested answers or completions. Select the one that is best in each case.

1. Probably the most famous moral-religious allegory was written in two parts, by John Bunyan. Its title is

    (A) *The Sound and the Fury*
    (B) *Aeropagitica*
    (C) *Tristram Shandy*
    (D) *Soliloquies*
    (E) *Pilgrim's Progress*

2. The protagonist of Dickens' *Bleak House* is a woman who catches smallpox, such that she becomes almost unrecognizable at the end of the book. The name of this Victorian heroin is

    (A) Emma
    (B) Esther
    (C) Jane
    (D) Marilyn
    (E) Alice

3. One of Jane Austen's novels deals with a young woman who the author tells us was not a good choice for "an heroine," and parodies such earlier Gothic novels as *The Mysteries of Udolpho* and *The Castle of Otranto*. Its title is

    (A) *Northanger Abbey*
    (B) *Emma*
    (C) *Pride and Prejudice*
    (D) *Far from the Madding Crowd*
    (E) *The Mill on the Floss*

4. In *Gulliver's Travels*, Lemuel Gulliver visits four main countries. The first place he travels to (or rather, is shipwrecked in) is

    (A) Taiwan
    (B) Ireland
    (C) Brobdingnag
    (D) Lilliput
    (E) Japan

5. Large, top-rounded windows, as well as aqueducts, are fine examples of what Roman contribution to architecture?

   (A) the arch
   (B) the post and lintel
   (C) the pyramid
   (D) the geodesic dome
   (E) the ziggurat

6. Over the centuries, the most important influence on architecture has been

   (A) sport
   (B) religion
   (C) drama
   (D) cooking
   (E) study

Questions 7-9 refer to the following literary works:

   I.   *The Iliad*
   II. *Hamlet*
   III. *Moby Dick*
   IV. *The Waste Land*
   V.   *The Faerie Queene*

7. The correct chronological order of the works listed above is

   (A) IV, III, II, I, V
   (B) I, II, III, IV, V
   (C) I, V, IV, III, II
   (D) I, V, II, III, IV
   (E) I, V, II, IV, III

8. Which is NOT written in verse?

   (A) I
   (B) II
   (C) III
   (D) IV
   (E) V

9. Which were written by American authors?

   (A) I, IV, and V
   (B) III only
   (C) III and IV
   (D) II, III and IV
   (E) II and III

10. The early English poem "Edward" is by

   (A) anonymous
   (B) Ernest Feneloso
   (C) Robert Frost
   (D) John Milton
   (E) Alfred A. Knopf

11. *H.M.S. Pinafore* and *The Pirates of Penzance* are operas by what famous lyricist-composer team?

    (A) Lerner and Lowe
    (B) Rogers and Bernstein
    (C) Rogers and Hammerstein
    (D) Gilbert and Sullivan
    (E) Lennon and McCartney

12. In musical notation, a bar is the same as

    (A) counterpoint
    (B) harmony
    (C) a clef
    (D) a staff
    (E) a measure

13. The portion of a story in which the plot is resolved is known as the

    (A) exposition
    (B) crescendo
    (C) doppleganger
    (D) denouement
    (E) falling action

14. The notion of evolution as discussed by Charles Darwin in *The Origin of Species* contains the seeds of what literary movement?

    (A) Augustanism
    (B) Romanticism
    (C) Pre-Romanticism
    (D) Realism
    (E) Empiricism

Questions 15-18 refer to the following excerpt:

> My song is arms and a man, the first of Troy to come to Italy and Lavinian shores, a fated fugitive, harried on land and sea by heaven's huge might and Juno's endless hate, pommeled by wars, till he could found the City and bring his gods to Latium, whence the race of Latins, our Alban sires, and towering Rome.

15. The person described in the passage is what literary figure?

    (A) Homer
    (B) Aeneas
    (C) Odysseus
    (D) Turnus
    (E) Priam

16. The author of the passage is

    (A) Cicero
    (B) Livy
    (C) Tacitus
    (D) Milton
    (E) Vergil

17. Juno (line four) is

    (A) a Trojan general
    (B) a Latin general
    (C) a Latin warrior
    (D) a Trojan god
    (E) a Roman goddess

18. The work from which the passage is taken is probably

    (A) an epic
    (B) a short story
    (C) didactic
    (D) symbolic
    (E) a religious play

Questions 19-21 refer to the following:

    I. *The Song of Roland*
    II. *Paradise Lost*
    III. *The Decameron*
    IV. *Beowulf*
    V. *The Divine Comedy*

19. Which are art epics?

    (A) I and IV
    (B) I and V
    (C) II and IV
    (D) III and IV
    (E) II and V

20. Which are folk epics?

    (A) II and IV
    (B) I and IV
    (C) III and V
    (D) III and IV
    (E) I and II

21. Which is NOT an epic?

    (A) I
    (B) II
    (C) III
    (D) IV
    (E) V

125

Questions 22-26 refer to the following paintings:

(A)

(B)

Courtesy Metropolitan Museum of Art
The H.O. Havemeyer Collection. Bequest
of Mrs. H.O. Havemeyer, 1929.

(C)

(D)

Courtesy Metropolitan Museum of Art, Wolfe Fund, 1906

(E)

22. Which is by Winslow Homer?

(A)
(B)
(C)
(D)
(E)

23. Which is Byzantine?

(A)
(B)
(C)
(D)
(E)

24. Which is by Monet?

(A)
(B)
(C)
(D)
(E)

25. Which is a realistic painting by Daumier?

    (A)
    (B)
    (C)
    (D)
    (E)

26. Which was probably painted in India?

    (A)
    (B)
    (C)
    (D)
    (E)

27. He allowed his ambition as general of the armies against Troy to override his love and duty as a father. To change the unfavorable winds sent by Artemis, he summoned his daughter Iphigenia, and sacrificed her. The tragic figure of Greek literature described above is

    (A) Agamemnon
    (B) Oedipus
    (C) Ajax
    (D) Achilles
    (E) Odysseus

28. Alexander Pope called an attempt at sublime expression which backfires and thus becomes silly

    (A) zeugma
    (B) pathos
    (C) bathos
    (D) tragedy
    (E) satire

29. Besides "Portrait of Mrs. Siddons," Gainsborough is best known for

    (A) "The Blue Boy"
    (B) "The Shrimp Girl"
    (C) "The Parson's Daughter"
    (D) "A Boy with a Rabbit"
    (E) "Portrait of Master Lambton"

30. This painter was born in France in 1444, and is best known for his painting of "The Birth of Venus." His name is

    (A) Sandro Botticelli
    (B) Leonardo da Vinci
    (C) Albertinelli
    (D) Pablo Picasso
    (E) Titian

131

31. The Platonic dialogue that deals with the origin of language (ironically) is

   (A) *Meno*
   (B) *Cratylus*
   (C) *Phaedo*
   (D) *Apology*
   (E) *Symposium*

32. In *The Republic*, Plato writes that, regarding poets, he would

   (A) not allow them into the republic
   (B) pay them to come to the republic
   (C) pay them to be part-time soldiers
   (D) allow them to come into the republic, but not pay them
   (E) force everyone to read their works

33. James Whistler painted not only a famous portrait of Thomas Carlyle, but also a portrait of

   (A) his father
   (B) his brother
   (C) his mother
   (D) Carlyle's mother
   (E) his dog

34. Nobody would ever say that William Butler Yeats was a BETTER poet then

   (A) Rod McKuen
   (B) Edgar Guest
   (C) Robert Lowell
   (D) William Shakespeare
   (E) Joyce Kilmer

35. This important literary movement, culminating in the works of Wordsworth, Coleridge and other early nineteenth century poets, had its roots in Milton and the Renaissance, and continued as an undercurrent of intellectual life throughout the eighteenth century in England. It includes such writers as Anthony Ashley Cooper (the Third Earl of Shaftesbury), the Warton Brothers (and possibly their father) and Thomas Gray. The name of the movement is

   (A) Pre-Romanticism
   (B) Augustanism
   (C) Neo-Classicism
   (D) Determinism
   (E) Criticism

36. Four beautiful pieces for the piano were written by Frederic Chopin and grouped under one generic name. Perhaps the most famous of them is in G minor. They are

   (A) *Etudes*
   (B) *Preludes*
   (C) *Mazurkas*
   (D) *Polonaises*
   (E) *Ballades*

37. Who was Ossian?

    (A) a poet of the nineteenth century
    (B) a pseudonym created as a hoax by Edgar Allen Poe
    (C) a pseudonym created as a hoax by James MacPherson
    (D) a friend of Samuel Johnson
    (E) a French contemporary of Chaucer

Questions 38-47 refer to the following sonnet:

> When in disgrace with fortune and men's eyes,
> I all alone beweep my outcast state
> And trouble deaf heaven with my bootless cries,
> And look upon myself and curse my fate,
> Wishing me like to one more rich in hope,
> Featur'd like him, like him with friends possess'd,
> Desiring this man's art and that man's scope,
> With what I most enjoy contented least,
> Yet in these thoughts myself almost despising,
> Haply I think on thee, and then my state,
> Like to the lark at break of day arising,
> From sullen earth sings hymns at heaven's gate,
> For thy sweet love rememb'red such wealth brings,
> That then I scorn to change my state with kings.

38. This sonnet is made up of

    (A) an octave and a sestet
    (B) three quatrains and a couplet
    (C) five couplets and a quatrain
    (D) four triplets and a couplet
    (E) fourteen lines of blank verse

39. Its rhyme scheme is

    (A) a-b-a-b-c-d-c-d-e-b-e-b-g-g
    (B) a-a-b-b-c-c-d-d-e-e-b-b-g-g
    (C) a-b-a-b-a-b-a-b-c-d-c-d-e-e
    (D) a-b-c-d-a-b-c-d-a-b-c-d-e-e
    (E) a-b-a-b-c-c-d-d-a-b-a-b-e-e

40. In line three, "bootless" means

    (A) barefoot
    (B) wailing
    (C) heedless
    (D) nervous
    (E) useless

41. In lines 10-11, the poet compares his "state" to "a lark." This poetic device is called

    (A) metaphor
    (B) synecdoche
    (C) exposition
    (D) iambic pentameter
    (E) simile

42. The author of this sonnet is

    (A)   William Shakespeare
    (B)   George Meredith
    (C)   Edmund Spenser
    (D)   Ben Jonson
    (E)   Petrarch

43. In line six, the poet employs both chiasmus and

    (A)   zeugma
    (B)   argumentum ad baculam
    (C)   repetition
    (D)   internal rhyme
    (E)   sprung rhythm

44. The meter of this poem is

    (A)   trochaic dimeter
    (B)   anapestic monometer
    (C)   iambic pentameter
    (D)   allegorical onomatpoeia
    (E)   iambic tetrameter

45. In line 10, the word "haply" means

    (A)   sadly
    (B)   happily
    (C)   doubtfully
    (D)   luckily
    (E)   hopefully

46. "Wishing me like to one more rich in hope" in line five is an example of

    (A)   simile
    (B)   metaphor
    (C)   onomatopoeia
    (D)   philosophy
    (E)   none of the above

47. Perhaps the most significant word in this poem is "state," which states the theme. In line 2-4, it is rhymed with fate. Why?

    (A)   because Shakespeare couldn't think of any other rhyme
    (B)   to rhyme with "gate" in line 12
    (C)   because the "state" was in trouble in England at the time
    (D)   because the poet's state is due to fate
    (E)   because of the mythological three fates

48. The composer of the "Hammerklavier Sonata" and the "Pastoral" and "Eroica" symphonies was

    (A)   Wolfgang Amadeus Mozart
    (B)   Ludwig von Beethoven
    (C)   Richard Wagner
    (D)   Sergei Rachmaninoff
    (E)   Walter Piston

Questions 49-53 refer to the following art work:

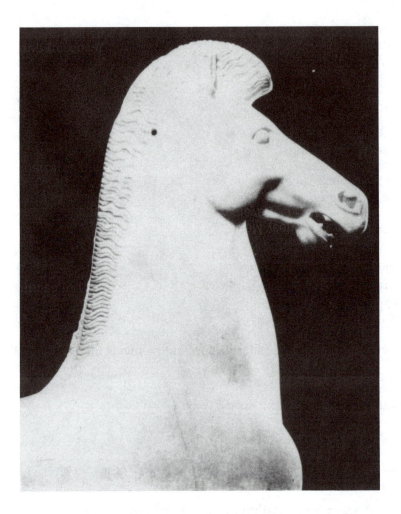

(A)

Courtesy the Metropolitan Museum of Art
Gift of Harry Payne Bingham, 1937.

(B)

Courtesy Metropolitan Museum of Art
Purchase, 1958, Fund from Various Donors.

(C)

(D)
Courtesy Metropolitan Museum of Art
Fletcher Fund 1940

(E)

138

49. Which contains frescoes?

   (A)
   (B)
   (C)
   (D)
   (E)

50. Which demonstrates the Greek attempt at realism?

   (A)
   (B)
   (C)
   (D)
   (E)

51. Which is Chinese in the style of Chou Fang?

   (A)
   (B)
   (C)
   (D)
   (E)

52. Which is by Peter Paul Rubens?

   (A)
   (B)
   (C)
   (D)
   (E)

53. Which is a famous statue of ancient Egypt?

   (A)
   (B)
   (C)
   (D)
   (E)

54. One of the great virtuosos of the piano in the nineteenth century, composer of *Concert Etudes*, was

   (A)   Van Cliburn
   (B)   Arthur Schnabel
   (C)   Vladimir Horowitz
   (D)   Franz Liszt
   (E)   Muzio Clementi

Questions 55-58 refer to the following persons:

    I. George Eliot
    II. George Sand
    III. George Gissing
    IV. George Meredith

55. Which of these are women?

    (A) I and II
    (B) III and IV
    (C) II and III
    (D) IV and II
    (E) none of the above

56. Which had a romantic relationship with composer Frederic Chopin?

    (A) IV
    (B) III
    (C) II
    (D) I
    (E) none of the above

57. Which wrote the sonnet cycle *Modern Love*?

    (A) IV
    (B) III
    (C) I
    (D) II
    (E) none of the above

58. Which wrote such famous novels as *Daniel Deronda* and *Middlemarch*?

    (A) II
    (B) I
    (C) III
    (D) IV
    (E) none of the above

59. The title of the utopia written by Francis Bacon, in which a group of explorers finds an island ruled by King Solamona, is

    (A) *Utopia*
    (B) *The Republic*
    (C) *Erewhon*
    (D) *New Atlantis*
    (E) *Walden II*

60. Montaigne, author of the *Essays*, is perhaps BEST known for his

    (A) skepticism
    (B) determinism
    (C) positivism
    (D) Platonism
    (E) phenomenology

61. "They hand in hand with wandering steps and slow, through Eden took their solitary way" are the closing lines of Milton's

   (A) "Lycidas"
   (B) *Comus*
   (C) *Samson Agonistes*
   (D) *Paradise Lost*
   (E) "Elegy Written in a Country Church-Yard"

62. The analysis of language based on its underlying or "deep" structure, begun by Noam Chomsky in the latter part of the twentieth century, results in

   (A) logical positivism
   (B) phonetics
   (C) phonemeics
   (D) phrase-structure grammar
   (E) transformational-generative grammar

63. A famous short story by Nathaniel Hawthorne deals with the allegorical religious theme of the role of Satan. It includes a trip through a forest to a meeting of witches. It is called

   (A) *The House of the Seven Gables*
   (B) *The Scarlet Letter*
   (C) "The Man Who Corrupted Hadleyburg"
   (D) "Young Goodman Brown"
   (E) "The Deserted Village"

64. A famous literary critic, a professor at Columbia University, who spent much of his career repudiating the "new criticism," was

   (A) Cleanth Brooks
   (B) Lionel Trilling
   (C) John Barth
   (D) Charles Scribner
   (E) Wayne Booth

Questions 65-71 refers to the following excerpt:

> The yellow fog that rubs its back upon the window-panes,
> The yellow smoke that rubs its muzzle on the window-panes
> Licked its tongue into the corners of the evening,
> Lingered upon the pools that stand in drains
> Let fall upon its back the soot that falls from chimneys,
> Slipped by the terrace, made a sudden leap,
> And seeing that it was a soft October night,
> Curled once about the house, and fell asleep.

65. The major metaphor employed in these lines compares fog to a

   (A) snake
   (B) ziggurat
   (C) cat
   (D) fish
   (E) religion

66. Another metaphor employed compares the night to a

    (A) room
    (B) street
    (C) sewer
    (D) fog
    (E) philosophy

67. The first two lines are characterized by

    (A) alliteration
    (B) metonymy
    (C) assimilation
    (D) liturgical repetition
    (E) many prepositions

68. The end rhyme probably occurs near the end of the stanza because

    (A) the poet was tired of writing lines that did not rhyme
    (B) he wanted to move the verbs closer to the end of the lines
    (C) he forgot that he was writing unrhymed verse
    (D) he wanted to speak about the joys of falling asleep on a soft October night
    (E) he wanted to give the stanza a sense of closure by rhyming

69. If one compares "sudden leap" with "fell asleep" he notes that the poet is employing "chiasmus," or crossing, because the grammatical pattern of the two phrases is

    (A) adverb-verb/verb-adverb
    (B) noun-verb/verb-noun
    (C) preposition-noun/noun-preposition
    (D) adverb-preposition/preposition-adverb
    (E) clause-phrase/phrase-clause

70. This poem is called "The Love Song of J. Alfred Prufrock," and it is by

    (A) William Shakespeare
    (B) Joan Marston
    (C) William Dean Howells
    (D) Ezra Pond
    (E) T. S. Eliot

71. In the context of the poem as a whole, we know that it is "a soft October night" because of Eliot's interest in

    (A) opera
    (B) violin
    (C) physics and the passing of time
    (D) the vegetation gods
    (E) Italian painters like Michelangelo

72. A great ideological movement in modern literary criticism is

    (A) hermenutics
    (B) structuralism
    (C) deconstruction
    (D) historical criticism
    (E) feminist criticism

142

73. The ancient symbol of poetic excellence is the

   (A) laurel
   (B) rose
   (C) hyacinth
   (D) amaranth
   (E) pansy

74. A famous writer of scurrilous satire and obscenely erotic verse at the court of Charles II was

   (A) the Earl of Rochester
   (B) Earl Shaftesbury
   (C) Robert Frost
   (D) the Duke of Marlborough
   (E) George II

75. Under this man's protectorate, all the theaters in England were closed, Charles I was beheaded, and his Latin secretary was John Milton. He was a Puritan, and his name was

   (A) William Penn
   (B) Lord North
   (C) Archbishop Laud
   (D) Oliver Cromwell
   (E) Thomas Cromwell

Questions 76-77 refer to the following lines:

> The Negro
> With the trumpet at his lips
> Whose jacket
> Has a <u>fine</u> one-button roll,
> Does not know
> Upon what riff the music slips
> Its hypodermic needle
> To his soul---

76. These lines are by a famous African American poet, who died in 1967. He was

   (A) Ralph Ellison
   (B) Langston Hughes
   (C) James Weldon Johnson
   (D) Paul Laurence Dunbar
   (E) Sterling A. Brown

77. The black man in the poem has a trumpet because

   (A) he is a symbol of an angel blowing a trumpet
   (B) he is trying to be like a white man
   (C) he is a slave
   (D) the poet liked music
   (E) of the close relationship of the black culture to jazz

78. What form of abstract art places emphasis on the use of cones and cubes?

(A) realism
(B) naturalism
(C) Renaissance
(D) dadaism
(E) cubism

Questions 79-81 refer to the following painting:

Courtesy Metropolitan Museum of Art,
Bequest of Mrs. H.O. Havemeyer, 1929.
The H.O. Havemeyer Collection.

144

79. The style of the painting is best described as

    (A) impressionistic
    (B) realistic
    (C) baroque
    (D) ugly
    (E) rococo

80. The painter was

    (A) da Vinci
    (B) d'Arezzo
    (C) Mormon
    (D) Fragonard
    (E) El Greco

81. The title of the painting is

    (A) "View of Toledo"
    (B) "Storm Warning"
    (C) "Before the Fall"
    (D) "Toledo and Towers"
    (E) "Approaching Toledo"

82. A pyramidical structure of ancient Mesopotamia used primarily as a high place for exercise of religion is known as

(A) a pyramid
(B) an acropolis
(C) a pagoda
(D) a temple
(E) a ziggurat

83. Of the following novels, which one was written by a woman?

(A) *Vanity Fair*
(B) *Silas Marner*
(C) *Great Expectations*
(D) *Moby Dick*
(E) *Nostromo*

84. One of the favorite musical instruments in Scotland is the

(A) harp
(B) piano
(C) dulcimer
(D) cello
(E) bagpipe

85. A dramatic entertainment presented by dancers in costume with musical accompaniment is a

(A) symphony
(B) ballet
(C) concerto
(D) chorale
(E) oratorio

86. A common instrument in early American black music is the

(A) piano
(B) lyre
(C) violin
(D) banjo
(E) clarinet

87. "Restoration comedy" is a term usually applied to the plays performed for the English aristocracy, beginning when theaters opened after the rule of the Puritans, in the reign of

(A) King Charles II
(B) King Charles I
(C) King George III
(D) Richard III
(E) King James I

> my father moved through dooms of love
> through sames of am through haves of give
> singing each morning out of each night
> my father moved through depths of height
>
> this motionless forgetful where   5
> turned at his glance to shining here;
> that if (so timid air is firm)
> under his eyes would stir and squirm
>
> newly as from unburied which
> floats the first who, his april touch   10
> drove sleeping selves to swarm their fates
> woke dreamers to their ghostly roots
>
> and should some why completely weep
> my father's fingers brought her sleep:
> vainly no smallest voice might cry   15
> for he could feel the mountains grow.

88. Line three is an expression of

    (A) optimism
    (B) music
    (C) happiness
    (D) pessimism
    (E) disgust

89. "Depths of height" in line four is

    (A) a simile
    (B) a metaphor
    (C) an oxymoron
    (D) an alliteration
    (E) a contradiction

90. "Woke dreamers to their ghostly roots" in line 12 means

    (A) the father prevented any more dreams
    (B) dreams are unattainable
    (C) dreams are not good for the father in the poem, or his acquaintances
    (D) the father helped others make their dreams reality
    (E) dreams are relegated to the psychiatrist

91. This poem was most likely written by

    (A) T. S. Eliot
    (B) George Bernard Shaw
    (C) Robert Blake
    (D) Lord Byron
    (E) E. E. Cummings

92. A percussion instrument characteristic of Latin music, consisting of shell-shaped pieces of wood, is called

    (A) bongos
    (B) tambourine
    (C) castanets
    (D) liberaces
    (E) taps

93. The unities, or principles of dramatic action set down by Aristotle, are

    (A) time, space and motion
    (B) time, place and action
    (C) rhyme, place and action
    (D) rhyme, place and interaction
    (E) consistency, space and interaction

94. Puck, Oberon and Titania are fairy characters from

    (A) *Peter Pan*
    (B) *The Faerie Queene*
    (C) *Charlotte's Web*
    (D) *A Midsummer Night's Dream*
    (E) *The Hobbit*

Questions 95-98 refer to the following lines:

> Thus sang the uncouth swain to the oaks and rills,
> While the still morn went out with sandals grey:
> He touched the tender stops of various quills,
> With eager thought warbling his Doric lay:
> And now the sun had stretched out all the hills,   5
> And now was dropt into the western bay;
> At last he rose, and twitched his mantle blew:
> To-morrow to fresh woods and pastures new.

95. These lines are from a poem commonly considered to be the greatest lyric poem in the English language, "Lycidas." Who is the poem's author?

    (A) Samuel Johnson
    (B) John Milton
    (C) William Shakespeare
    (D) Ben Jonson
    (E) Edmund Spenser

96. In the context of the fourth line, what does the word "Doric" mean?

    (A) pastoral
    (B) military
    (C) Greek
    (D) iambic
    (E) Byzantine

97. The poem as a whole is one of the best-known examples of what literary form?

   (A) satire
   (B) mock epic
   (C) elegy
   (D) epistle
   (E) ballad

98. The poetic foot employed in the poem is the

   (A) trochee
   (B) spondee
   (C) iamb
   (D) dactyl
   (E) anapest

Questions 99-100 refer to the following photograph:

99. This ancient building is known as

    (A) the coliseum
    (B) the agora
    (C) the Parthenon
    (D) the forum
    (E) the acropolis

100. The columns, which once supported elaborate friezes and a large roof, can best be described as

    (A) massive
    (B) Doric
    (C) Corinthian
    (D) marble
    (E) Ionic

101. Cello, the name of a musical instrument, is an abbreviation of

    (A) bass cello
    (B) alto cello
    (C) tympani cello
    (D) soprano cello
    (E) violincello

102. An orchestral suite written by Handel to celebrate a royal occasion on the Thames is called

    (A) *The Water Music*
    (B) *A Little Night Music*
    (C) the "Eroica"
    (D) *A Hero's Life*
    (E) *Moll Flanders*

103. This collection of preludes and fugues was written by Bach, with one piece in each of the major and minor keys, partly in order to change the practice in tuning of pianos to the use of "equal temperament." It is called

    (A) *Equal temperament*
    (B) *Preludes and Fugues*
    (C) *The Hammerklavier*
    (D) *The Well Tuned Clavier*
    (E) *The Etudes*

104. A musical composition in three or more parts in which the parts enter in succession and use the same melody and words, sing as many phrases as there are parts, and return to the first phrase is the

    (A) sonata
    (B) symphony
    (C) rock lyric
    (D) round
    (E) ballad

105. Three-part (exposition, development, recapitulation) form in music is known as

    (A)   triptych form
    (B)   triglyph form
    (C)   trinity form
    (D)   trimeter form
    (E)   sonata form

Questions 106-108 refer to the following lines:

> And did those feet in ancient time
> Walk upon England's mountains green?
> And was the Holy Lamb of God
> On England's pleasant pastures seen?

106. These lines are by William Blake, from his poem "Milton." They are also the lyrics of a rock song by what group?

    (A)   Emerson, Lake and Palmer
    (B)   The Beatles
    (C)   Crosby, Stills, Nash and Young
    (D)   Santana
    (E)   The Partridge Family

107. The "Holy Lamb of God" in the poem is

    (A)   Mahomet
    (B)   Jesus Christ
    (C)   Milton
    (D)   Oliver Cromwell
    (E)   Mary

108. When he invokes the presence of a man by reference to the character's feet in the first line, the poet employs a rhetorical device in which the part is taken for the whole, called

    (A)   zeugma
    (B)   chiasmus
    (C)   exposition
    (D)   synechodoche
    (E)   metonymy

109. In the theatres of Shakespeare's time, the wealthy people sat on the stage or in the balconies. Commoners sat in the

    (A)   mezzanine
    (B)   lobby
    (C)   outside, because they were not allowed "inside"
    (D)   pit
    (E)   booths in the back of the auditorium

110. Elizabethan theatres are believed to have evolved from

   (A) haylofts
   (B) stables
   (C) church steps
   (D) sports stadia
   (E) medieval inns

111. The most famous of theatres in which Shakespeare's plays were produced in Elizabethan London was

   (A) The World
   (B) The Strand
   (C) The Midway
   (D) The Globe
   (E) The Carnival

112. Which of the following is NOT an actor?

   (A) George Orwell
   (B) Laurence Olivier
   (C) Richard Burton
   (D) Sir John Gielgud
   (E) Marlon Brando

113. Which of the following is NOT known for his piano performances?

   (A) Vladimir Horowitz
   (B) Rudolph Serken
   (C) Virgil Fox
   (D) Van Cliburn
   (E) none of the above

114. Shakespeare and Ben Jonson, with their contemporaries, are usually thought of as Renaissance, Elizabethan, or, sometimes,

   (A) Jacobean
   (B) Romantic
   (C) Restoration
   (D) Augustan
   (E) Neo-Platonist

Questions 115-117 refer to the following persons:

    I.   Beverly Sills
   II.   Janis Ian
  III. Leontyne Price
  IV. Ethel Merman
   V. Lily Pons

115.   Which are known for their excellence as operatic soloists?

    (A)   I, II and III
    (B)   I, III and IV
    (C)   I, III and V
    (D)   II, III and V
    (E)   I, II and V

116.   Which is known for her award-winning popular music of the mid-70s?

    (A)   I
    (B)   II
    (C)   III
    (D)   IV
    (E)   V

117.   Which is known for her Broadway musical performances, particularly in *Annie Get Your Gun?*

    (A)   III
    (B)   IV
    (C)   I
    (D)   II
    (E)   V

118.   Nave, narthex and sanctuary are parts of

    (A)   a coliseum
    (B)   a library
    (C)   a train station
    (D)   a triumphal arch
    (E)   a cathedral

119.   The first free-standing statue in history, a creation reminiscent of Michelangelo's *David* but with military boots and hat, is

    (A)   Puccini's *David*
    (B)   Botticelli's *David*
    (C)   Donatello's *David*
    (D)   Van Eyck's *David*
    (E)   Rodan's *The Thinker*

120. This old tale is the subtext of works by several authors, including Chaucer and Shakespeare. It is

    (A)   Antonio and Melida
    (B)   Romeo and Juliet
    (C)   Troilus and Cressida
    (D)   Artemis and Gordon
    (E)   Daphnis and Chloe

Questions 121-123 refer to the following illustration:

121. The two fours, written as a fraction in the musical notation, are known as the

    (A)   time fraction
    (B)   beat
    (C)   rhythm
    (D)   time signature
    (E)   key signature

122. The figure drawn all the way to the left on the staff is

    (A)   a half note
    (B)   treble clef
    (C)   without significance
    (D)   for female vocalists
    (E)   key signature

123. From the information given in the illustration, one knows that

    (A)   the music following is written in three sharps
    (B)   female vocalists will be unable to reach the low pitches
    (C)   the music following will be in S major
    (D)   the rhythm is cut time
    (E)   the music is intended for instrumental playing only

124. In its functionalist application, Bauhaus architecture in Germany was similar to the "machines a habiter" of

    (A)   Gibbons in England
    (B)   DeGaulle in France
    (C)   Marx in Ukrania
    (D)   Le Corbusier in France
    (E)   Picasso in Spain

125. Which of the following is a famous fresco?

    (A) "Mona Lisa"
    (B) "Giovanni Arnolfini and His Bride"
    (C) "The School of Athens"
    (D) "Washington Crossing the Delaware"
    (E) "The Birth of Venus"

126. The artist who painted "Washington Crossing the Delaware" is

    (A) Arthur Fiedler
    (B) Eugene Ormandy
    (C) Andrew Wyeth
    (D) Norman Rockwell
    (E) Emanuel Leutze

Questions 127-130 refer to illustrations (A)-(E):

(A)

156

(B)

(C)

157

(D)

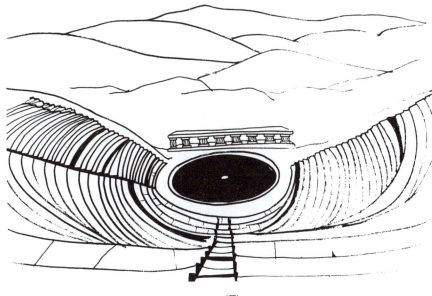

(E)

127. The theme of painting (A) is

    (A) belligerent
    (B) bellicose
    (C) restrictive
    (D) religious
    (E) sacreligious

128. Which structure probably employs flying buttresses?

    (A)
    (B)
    (C)
    (D)
    (E)

129. Which structure can be best described as Romanesque?

    (A)
    (B)
    (C)
    (D)
    (E)

130. Which is Byzantine?

    (A)
    (B)
    (C)
    (D)
    (E)

Questions 131-135 refer to the following composers:

    I. Wagner
    II. Vivaldi
    III. Stravinsky
    IV. Bruckner
    V. Debussy

131. Which is known for his Renaissance concertos and choral compositions?

    (A) III
    (B) II
    (C) V
    (D) I
    (E) IV

132. Which composed The Rite of Spring and The Fire Bird?

    (A) I
    (B) II
    (C) III
    (D) V
    (E) IV

133. Which was Austrian?

   (A) I
   (B) II
   (C) III
   (D) IV
   (E) V

134. Which wrote *Der Ring des Nibelungen*?

   (A) V
   (B) IV
   (C) III
   (D) II
   (E) I

135. Which composed "Clair de Lune"?

   (A) IV
   (B) III
   (C) II
   (D) I
   (E) V

136. Bertolt Brecht and Kurt Weill collaborated to produce a musical play about a fictional character, Mack the Knife, called

   (A) *The Threepenny Opera*
   (B) *Three Coins in the Fountain*
   (C) *Fountain of Youth*
   (D) *The Caucasian Chalk Circle*
   (E) *Mother Courage*

137. Nationalism, as expressed in the *1812 Overture*, is a recurrent theme of the Russian composer

   (A) Tchaikovsky
   (B) Marx
   (C) Stravinsky
   (D) Copland
   (E) Strauss

138. One nineteenth century American poet, who lived in Amherst, Massachusetts, was denigrated as "diminutive" by male critics, until re-evaluated by modern revisionist feminist critics. The poet was

   (A) Walt Whitman
   (B) Willa Cather
   (C) Emily Dickinson
   (D) Diana Trilling
   (E) Joyce Kilmer

Questions 139-145 refer to the following passage:

In the late summer of that year we lived in a house in a village that looked across the river and the plain to the mountains. In the bed of the river there were pebbles and there were boulders, dry and white in the sun, and the water was clear and swiftly moving and blue in the channels. Troops went by the house and down the road and the dust they raised powdered the leaves of the trees. The trunks of the trees too were dusty and the leaves fell early that year and we saw the troops marching along the road and the dust rising and the leaves, stirred by the breeze, falling and the soldiers marching and afterward the road bare and white except for the leaves.

139. This passage is the opening paragraph of a novel by

   (A) Ernest Hemingway
   (B) Henry David Thoreau
   (C) James A. Michener
   (D) Philip Roth
   (E) Theodore Dreiser

140. The rest of the novel is probably about

   (A) baseball
   (B) the American West
   (C) a man who is kidnapped by a gang of Italian terrorists
   (D) fishing
   (E) war

141. The river in the second sentence is probably a symbol of

   (A) the house
   (B) the philosophy of John Locke
   (C) the flowing events of life
   (D) the movement of Huck and Jim toward freedom
   (E) the leaves from the trees

142. A symbol parallel to that of the river is the

   (A) leaves
   (B) house
   (C) pebbles
   (D) road
   (E) water

143. The pebbles in the streams are much like

   (A) leaves on the trees
   (B) troops in the road
   (C) people in the house
   (D) leaves in the road
   (E) all of the above

144. The leaves probably happen to be falling off the trees

    (A)   only because it is autumn
    (B)   only because of the dust raised by the soldiers
    (C)   only because of the lack of water in the stream
    (D)   for the same reason that it is "a soft October night" in "The Love Song of J. Alfred Prufrock"
    (E)   only because leaves fall early in Europe

145. If you think about its relationship to history, the prose style of this passage best reflects

    (A)   the social consciousness that led to manifest destiny
    (B)   the social consciousness that led to the Emancipation Proclamation
    (C)   the saddened social consciousness after the assassination of John F. Kennedy
    (D)   the memories of a suffragette
    (E)   the shell-shocked, post-World War I social consciousness

Questions 146-150 refer to the following lines:

> Cast a cold eye
> On life, on death.
> Horseman, pass by!

146. These words are cut into the tombstone of their author, the Irish poet

    (A)   Jonathan Swift
    (B)   Oliver Goldsmith
    (C)   Flannery O'Connor
    (D)   William Butler Yeats
    (E)   Hugh McDairmid

147. The lines are from his "death" poem, "Under Ben Bulben." In the rest of the poem he instructs

    (A)   Irish poets and painters
    (B)   school children
    (C)   spirits of the mountains
    (D)   the English king
    (E)   the Irish parliament

148. A "ben" in the context of the poem is

    (A)   lake
    (B)   man's name
    (C)   curve in a river
    (D)   mountain
    (E)   kind of mythological tree

149. The lines quoted above are sentences written in which voice?

    (A)   declarative
    (B)   interrogative
    (C)   exclamatory
    (D)   passive
    (E)   imperative

150.   The third line employs the rhetorical technique of

     (A)   exposition
     (B)   denouement
     (C)   opposition
     (D)   "posing"
     (E)   antithesis

ANSWERS AND EXPLANATIONS
SAMPLE EXAMINATION II
SECTION I

1. **(E)** Clearly a story that operates on the physical level of the characters but at the same time representing abstract ideas, *Pilgrim's Progress* is the story of a man, Christian, who journeys through the Slough of Despond and Vanity Fair on the way to his salvation.

2. **(B)**

3. **(A)** *Northanger Abbey* pokes fun at the popular Gothic novels of the late 18th and early 19th centuries in England. Of the remaining choices, *Emma* and *Pride and Prejudice* are two of Austen's best efforts, but they have nothing to do with parodies or Gothic novels.

4. **(D)** The Lilliputians were tiny people, and a vehicle for Swift's social satire of 18th century England and Ireland. When Gulliver washes up, unconscious, on the shores of Lilliput, the little people attempt to tie the "giant" up and stake him to the ground.

5. **(A)** While there were few Roman advances in art, the semicircular arch, seen in windows, aqueducts and bridges, was a great and important contribution to architecture. Ancient Greece invented the post and lintel; Egypt the pyramid; and Mesopotamia the ziggurat. The American, R. Buckminster Fuller, invented the geodesic dome.

6. **(B)** From the Egyptians, who built pyramids to bury the pharaohs, through the Mesopotamians, whose ziggurats provided high places for worship in a flat land, on through Greek temples and Roman medieval churches, religion has motivated and influenced building more than any other cause.

7. **(D)** It is estimated that *The Iliad*, apparently by Homer, was written around 1,000 B.C. Spenser first published *The Faerie Queene* in 1590, and Hamlet appeared in 1603. Melville's *Moby Dick* came out in America in 1851, while Eliot's long poem in five parts, *The Waste Land*, was published in 1922.

8. **(C)** *Moby Dick*, a long novel of whaling, is the only work of the five not in verse. *The Iliad* is usually seen in English in iambic pentameter, and *Hamlet*, as all of Shakespeare's plays, is in the same meter. *The Waste Land* is free verse, while *The Faerie Queene* is Spenserian stanza (rhyme scheme: ababbcbcc).

9. **(C)** Melville, who wrote choice III, *Moby Dick*, lived in New England. Eliot, author of IV, *The Waste Land*, spent most of his life in England and actually became a British citizen. However, since he was born in the United States, Eliot is regarded as an American author.

10. **(A)**

11. **(D)**

12. **(E)** The two terms are synonymous, though measure is more formal.

13. **(D)** Denouement is the same as climax: the action comes to its resolution or high point. Falling action (E) follows the denouement, while exposition usually opens a literary work.

14. (D) Darwin's theory caused writers to take a look at the world from a new perspective, one of survival of the fittest and man in relation to his environment. Realism is an outgrowth of that new viewpoint.

15. (B) This may be the best seven-line description of the founder of the Roman race from Vergil's *Aeneid*. It contains his origin, geographical destination, and fate.

16. (E)

17. (E) Juno, the queen of the gods, was antagonistic to Troy from the time a Trojan chose Venus over her to be most fair. Of course, that action took place in Homer's epic, *The Iliad*, in which Juno was called by her Greek name, Hera, and Venus by hers, Aphrodite.

18. (A) We can tell, without knowing specifically that the work is *The Aeneid*, that it is a selection from an epic. The passage is written in verse, describes a main character involved in heroic struggles and mixed up with the gods. All of the lines present the beginning of a story told in lofty language. These clues indicate that the work following is an epic.

19. (E) Because we have definite knowledge that Milton wrote *Paradise Lost* and Dante *The Divine Comedy*, these epics are known as art epics. Any epic of definite authorship is an art epic.

20. (B) *The Song of Roland and Beowulf*, like folk tales, cannot be historically attributed to a specific author. Therefore, we refer to them as folk epics.

21. (C) Boccacio's collection of stories is not an epic.

22. (E) Winslow Homer is especially known for his paintings of sea-related scenes. This one is "The Gulf Stream."

23. (D) Stiff, formal figures in unnatural poses make this icon of the Byzantine style. It is called "The Doubt of St. Thomas." You may recognize the characters from Bible stories.

24. (B) The painting is entitled "Women Seated Under the Willows."

25. (C) Daumier's painting "The Third Class Carriage" is called realistic because it depicts everyday people in a commonplace setting and attempts to portray them as in life.

26. (A) This painting, "Krishna and Radha," is a Hindu religious painting.

27. (A)

28. (C) Bathos is a play on the word pathos.

29. (A) "The Blue Boy" may be the more famous of the two Gainsborough paintings.

30 (A) Botticelli created "The Birth of Venus."

31. (B)

32. (A) Indeed, Plato said he would not permit poets into his utopia because of their disruptive influence.

33. (C) The painting, of course, is "Whistler's Mother."

34. (D) Shakespeare is generally held the greatest writer of English ever. While some scholars may believe there are poets as great as Shakespeare, none would say there was a better one.

35. (A) Wordsworth and Coleridge were romantic period poets, so certainly the period that preceded them would be Pre-Romanticism when all the other choices are considered.

36. (E)

37. (C)

38. (B)

39. (A)

40. (E)

41. (E) Remember that the key words in determining whether the comparison is a simile or a metaphor are "like" and "as."

42. (A)

43. (C)

44. (C) If the answer to this question is not obvious to you, reread the section on fundamentals of poetry. Try to diagram the lines to determine the meter.

45. (D) "Haply" and "happily," while from the same root, have entirely different meanings.

46. (E) The question is a tricky one, because it plays on your readiness to respond to any phrase with "like" or "as" in it with simile. In truth, it is not a simile because no comparison between two normally unrelated objects is made.

47. (D) This is the only logical response to question 47. There is no basis in the text for any of the others, while there is a basis for statement (D).

48. (B) Beethoven wrote all of these works. Those familiar with Beethoven's nine symphonies, which are certainly among his most important works, would have recognized "Pastoral."

49. (D) The paintings on the walls of King Tut's tomb are by definition frescoes.

50. (A) This representation of a horse from the Acropolis is an example of the successful Greek work toward natural lines in statues.

51. (E) The work is entitled "Play With Infants."

52. (B) This painting, with full-figured characters and obviously bold colors and shadows, is Rubens' "Venus and Adonis."

53. (C)

54. (D) Liszt is the only one of the five choices to have composed in the 19th century. The others are 20th century musicians.

55. (A) George Eliot was the pen name for the female British novelist, Mary Ann Evans. George Sand, literally so named, exerted personal influence over composer Chopin.

56. (C)

57. (A)

58. (B)

59. (D) The genre referred to as utopia is one in which the book describes an ideal world, usually according to the author's philosophy.

60. (A) Montaigne is known as the creator of the modern essay as a literary form. The skepticism expressed in his essays is religious in nature.

61. (D) *Paradise Lost* tells, simultaneously, the stories of Adam and Eve's fall from grace, and the battle for control of heaven between God and Jesus on one side and Lucifer on the other.

62. (E) Chomsky's understanding of language through this theory is that traditional laws of grammar and syntax achieve their correctness through use and disuse of a particular people and time.

63. (D) The reader should know immediately that (A) and (B) cannot be the answer, because they are italicized. Such treatment is not given to short stories, which are always placed in quotation marks. Books, novels and very long poems are underlined or italicized in print. Of course, were the reader familiar with Hawthorne's story, and this one he should know, he would not need to narrow the possible choices to (C), (D) and (E).

64. (B) Brooks, Barth, and Booth are all members of the school referred to here as new criticism. Trilling, however, opposes the psychological analysis new criticism applies. Scribner was a famous publisher, not a literary critic.

65. (C) From rubbing its back, licking its tongue, rubbing its muzzle, leaping suddenly, slipping by the terrace, curling once about the house and falling asleep, it is fairly obvious that the fog is being compared to a cat in these lines.

66. (A) See line seven.

67. (D) Simply the repetition of adjectives and verbs in this line tips the reader off to the correct answer. Repetition of such in the same construction in successive sentences comprises liturgical repetition. None of the other possible answers is logically supported by the text.

68. (E) The last choice is a logical one, and a reading of the quote lends support to it. The remaining answers are nonsensical.

69. (A)

70. (E) Other famous Eliot poems, also in free verse, include "The Hollow Men" and *The Waste Land*.

71. (D) Answering this question requires some background knowledge of the author. Most CLEP students would not be expected to answer question 71.

72. (E) The key word in this question is "ideological," for feminist criticism, unlike the others listed here, applies its ideological framework to analysis of literature. The others base their analyses on non-dogmatic bases, such as linguistics and history.

73. (A) One need only recall that England called its greatest living poet during his lifetime "the poet laureate" to answer this question.

74. (A) Rochester's stories and verse are ribald and quite funny to modern audiences, but were considered vulgar and tasteless in his day. This is a question CLEP students would not be expected to answer.

75. (D) Cromwell, while a historical figure, imposed himself upon the literary world and its history from 1649-1658 when he gained control of England by beheading Charles I. When he died nine years later, his son could not keep control of the country, and the English citizenry welcomed the reign of Charles II. The period following the end of Cromwell's puritanical rule is known as the Restoration.

76. (B)   The poem is "The Trumpet Player."

77. (E)   The relationship between African-American culture and music pre-dates the Emancipation Proclamation and has become a symbol of black philosophy and state of mind.

78. (E)   The object of cubism is to create pictures solely from the use of cones and cubes.

79. (C)   The contrast of light and shadow, as well as the use of bold, even unnatural, colors, makes this painting baroque in style.

80. (E)   El Greco, a Spaniard, painted in the baroque period and baroque style.

81. (A)

SECTION 2

82. (E)

83. (B)   *Silas Marner* was written by George Eliot, who was in reality a woman.

84. (E)   Of all these instruments, the bagpipe certainly arouses the strongest national feeling in the Scottish.

85. (B)   Only (B) can be a correct choice. All the other answers are nonsensical.

86. (D)   While it is possible to argue that the violin was played by early American black musicians, the banjo was far more common in black music.

87. (A)   See question 75.

88. (A)   Singing is a positive action, and singing light out of dark can only be described as optimism.

89. (C)

90. (D)

91. (E)   The Cummings trademark is exclusive use of lower case letters. One will never find a capital letter in a Cummings poem.

92. (C)

93. (B)   The idea behind Aristotle's unities was to make each play a logical whole, by requiring all the action to occur in one place during one 24-hour period.

94. (D)

95. (B)

96. (A)

97. (C)   "Lycidas" is not a comic poem, so (A) and (B) are obviously incorrect. Since the poem is not a letter, (D) is eliminated. The length, language, and form prevent it from being a ballad.

98. (C)

99. (C)   The Parthenon was a temple to Pallas Athena, the patron goddess of the ancient Greek city, Athens. A coliseum is, of course, a circular stadium. An agora is a large, square, open marketplace, while a forum is a meeting place for public speaking and listening. The acropolis is the actual mount or highplace in a Greek city where that city's temple was placed. Hence, in Athens the Parthenon is built upon the acropolis.

100. (B) The capitals of the columns are plain, and thus Doric. The Corinthian style included elaborately decorated capitals; the Ionic consisted of a simple, curling decoration on each side.

101. (E)

102. (A) The Thames is the river flowing through London, where Handel spent most of his life. (B) is a Broadway musical. (C) is a symphony by Beethoven.

103. (D)

104. (D) Perhaps the best known round in America is "Row, Row, Row Your Boat." Apply it to the description in this question to better understand how the round works.

105. (E)

106. (A) The rock lyric is receiving ever greater attention as a literary form.

107. (B) All the imagery in this selection is Christian, hence (B).

108. (D)

109. (D) Such theaters were open air structures modeled after medieval inns. Because they sat or stood in the courtyard or ground portion, commoners at plays were often referred to as "groundlings."

110. (E)

111. (D) The Globe, functional models of which have been constructed in Stratford-on-Avon and the Folger Shakespeare Library in Washington, D.C., was the most famous.

112. (A) Orwell is a novelist. He wrote *1984*.

113. (C) Fox is known as one of the world's greatest organists.

114. (A) All these terms refer to the same period in English drama. (B), (C), (D) and (E) have no relation whatsoever to Shakespeare and his contemporaries.

115. (C)

116. (B)

117. (B)

118. (E) The nave is the seating area for the congregation. The narthex is the entrance to the cathedral behind the nave. The sanctuary contains the altar and is raised above the level of the congregation.

119. (C)

120. (C) Both Chaucer and Shakespeare wrote works by the same title. The other choices are not actual tales.

121. (D)

122. (B) A clef, in this case a treble clef, is the first thing to appear on a staff of music.

123. (A) One knows that the music is written in three sharps, because the three sharps drawn on the staff constitute the key signature.

124. (D) Both Bauhaus architects and Le Corbusier sought to combine function with artistic statement. Le Corbusier later in his life rejected this philosophy.

125. (C) The others are paintings. A fresco is a painting on a wall.

126. (E)

127. (D) The painting depicts the Virgin Mary and Jesus with Saint Anne. Surely, then, the tone is religious.

128. (B) The flying buttress was commonly employed in the building of Gothic cathedrals. It had artistic and functional purposes.

129. (D) Romanesque architecture was an attempt at recapturing the grand Roman style (which is still very Greek) while combining it with function in public buildings. Depicted here is St. Paul's Cathedral in London.

130. (C) Pictured here is St. Sophia's Cathedral in Istanbul.

131. (B)

132. (C)

133. (D)

134. (E)

135. (E)

136. (A)

137. (A) The *1812 Overture* was calculated to raise patriotic feelings in the Russian audience.

138. (C) Recent feminist emphasis on the works of Dickinson has elevated her works to the level of the greatest poems of American authors.

139. (A) In its simplicity of vocabulary and description, and its forthright manner, the passage is unmistakably Hemingway's. It is the opening section of *A Farewell to Arms*.

140. (E) The passage begins talking about natural beauty of the setting, but is quickly interrupted by the appearance of troops and their effect on the natural setting.

141. (C) A river is recognized throughout literature as a symbol of passing time and life.

142. (D) The "road of life" is almost a cliché as a saying, but it is a recognized literary symbol.

143. (A)

144. (D) See questions 65-71.

145. (E)

146. (D) They are perhaps the most famous lines Yeats wrote, and point up one of his most important philosophical questions, that of the relationship between life, death and art.

147. (A)

148. (D) Ben Bulben is a mount.

149. (E) The sentences command, thus they are written in the imperative voice.

150. (E)

You have now completed your review for the CLEP humanities examination. Check your answers and review the areas in which you are still having difficulty. Remember to be alert for material that falls into the humanities category as you read, watch television, or listen to the radio.